I
send
a voice

Cover and title page art by Terry Doerzaph
Illustrations by Narca Schor

I
send
a voice

by Evelyn Eaton

Quest Books

This publication made possible with the assistance of the Kern Foundation.
The Theosophical Publishing House
Wheaton, Ill./Madras, India/London, England

First Quest Book edition 1978
Fourth Quest printing 1987
published by the
Theosophical Publishing House, Wheaton, Illinois
a department of
The Theosophical Society
in America

Library of Congress Cataloging in Publication Data

Eaton, Evelyn Sybil Mary, 1902-1983
    I send a voice

    (A Quest book original)
    1. Eaton, Evelyn Sybil Mary, 1902-1983 – Religion and
ethics. 2. Authors, American – 20th century – Biography.
3. Indians of North America – California – Religion and
mythology.   I. Title.
PS3509.A84Z465   813'.5'2 (B)   78-7273
ISBN 0-8356-0513-2
ISBN 0-8356-0511-6 pbk.

Printed in the United States of America

For Dr. Gayle

Nilum pesazmuk elintaquk.
(Micmac)

[We are the stars which sing.]

Author's Note

My gratitude goes to the Marsden Foundation, whose award made possible the time spent in research and writing this sharing of a personal experience which I hope may be a bridge between travellers on different paths, leading to the Center.

My grateful thanks also go to the three Medicine Men whom I refer to as *Tsaviaya, Power Man* and *Eagle Man*, as I refer to their families and other friends by pseudonyms or initials. The political climate has changed since 1965 when I was first taken into the Sweats and Ceremonies and given the Pipe, and since I was urged to write the book. There is now a need, some Indians feel, *not* to be considered friendly to non-Indians, especially concerning sacred ways.

When we meet alone, or in the Sweat Lodges, we revert to the old warmth, knowing that the Grandfathers do not judge by pigmentation, but in public (and a book is public) the best gift a non-Indian can proffer to Indian friends, as of 1977, is a self-imposed restraint. When the picture changes, the names of the Medicine Men and the others who wanted me to write this book and offered me their help, may be revealed.

It is not written chronologically. I have grouped together the Sweats, the Fasts, the Pipe, Dances, and other training experiences, though these were happening concurrently. It is intended to be a "Give-away" present to both races.

Evelyn Eaton
(Ma'ha dyuni)

I SEND A VOICE

Contents

Introduction

I have been asked to write this account of the training and work of a present-day Pipe-Woman because the time has come to reveal this way to those who *will* to take it. It is not necessary to be Amerindian, or part-Indian, or to offer oneself to be a Pipe-Woman, or to follow the Indian way, or any other way exclusively, in order to understand and undertake the great Journey.

> "Many roads Thou hast fashioned,
> All of them lead to the light"

from the well-defined, much travelled highroads of the great orthodox religions, to the little backroads and byways of individual approach. At one time or another, when the time is right, we encounter them, cross them, or enter them, outgrow and leave them, to travel further.

The first essential is to *want*. When we arrive at wanting, we know there is Something to be wanted. When we know that, we realize that there must be a bridge between want and Wanted, and we set out to find it. We start on a further stage of the road we have been travelling, consciously or unconsciously, "since time began", — which, of course, time doesn't, neither does it end.

The next essential is to start from where we are, in the shower, on the street, in the kitchen, in the office, on the plane, in the subway, in the desert, in the crowd, or alone. We have no need to go to Tibet, India, or the top of Mount Shasta. We are where we should be, now.

Now is the immediacy, *now* is the immortal moment, *now* is all the time we have. We have no power over the before-now which has brought us here, we do have power over the after-now, through what we do or don't do, *now*.

Here on the rim of the Great Medicine Wheel, mandala of the world, whose center is everywhere and circumference nowhere, we sound our horn, we send our voice, we cry our being's whole desire, or as Tsaviaya advised, "sit down where you are and set up a squawk. The Grandfathers hear. But you must *ask*."

If we ask aright, with integrity and total commitment, the way will be revealed, step by gentle step. So it is for me, so it is for you, so it is for everyone.

1

The *now* of 1965, the then-and-there that I was living through when a new turn of the road began, found me undergoing the preparation which traditionally precedes an enlargement of consciousness.

Now, as in the days of the Mystery Schools, the candidate for enlightenment who comes properly prepared, comes blindfold, in a state of darkness and uncertainty, a temporary withdrawal of vision, and comes unarmed, deprived of metals and valuables, that is those assets, tangible, intangible, which we set store by and rely on for protection and for power.

Metals, among their many meanings, represent the seven deadly sins, to us more than seven, if we take the newer metals of the 20th century, uranium, radium, plutonium, etc., misuse of atomic power, misuse of creative power, new enormous crimes against life itself.

13

We are told that we must be prepared first in our hearts, by wholehearted commitment to the Journey, then stripped of power, pride, greed and the other encumbrances before we can be said to come properly prepared. We must renounce, not material possessions so much as our dependence on them, and return in spirit, sometimes in fact, to simplicity, to harmlessness. We must have mastered our passions, or be trying to, especially pride in the exercise of power. We must be "poor in spirit", without attachment to material things.

The necessity of freedom from reliance upon metals, valuables, and all they represent, is stressed at every turn of the road. We are called upon to demonstrate our freedom, and if unable to satisfy the Challengers that we come properly prepared, Life, the great Initiator, repeats the challenge until we can and do pass the tests.

This does not mean that we must necessarily find ourselves suddenly bankrupt, starving, thrown out of our jobs or our homes, because we ask for Light, unless such seeming calamities are needed to break our dependence upon this-plane material power. The preparation is *symbolic* of the state of our consciousness at the time of asking, though it can also be actual, as it was with me.

In 1965, when this way began for me, I was living in a hut in the desert between two mountain ranges in California. Built by an old miner in 1915 it had neither electricity nor running water. There was no telephone, no bathroom. There were two gas jets, and a burning gas stove on one side, wood and trash in the other. A stream ran by the door. It was man-controlled, so that sometimes I came out to find it gone, and sometimes in the night woke to find it running strongly, singing as it went. There were old locust trees along the banks, whose fragrance drenched the air in spring, in summer they gave shade and privacy from a road too near. In the miner's day this was a seldom travelled path to the mountains, in mine a paved and busy highway.

The house was poorly furnished, with odds and ends mostly from the dump. I had emptied my savings — $375 — to buy it. I had an old jalopy and a loan of $600 which I was trying to live on for a year. At times there was little to eat, but I kept a rooster and two bantam hens, who between them gave me an egg every day. I grew vegetables in a patch behind the house. I gathered wild asparagus, dandelions, plants and other edibles the Indians showed me.

Also people came to me for help, a paper to be typed, advice on how to deal with establishment forms to be filled, or simple healing of little miseries. They sometimes brought me food. It was a time of deprivation which had come upon me suddenly, unforeseeably, two years before, the loss of a job, loss of health in my overcoat, yet it was a serene and growing time, a time of preparation.

Mostly we don't recognize these times for what they are until the experience for which we are being prepared is under way. I did not, in my three-dimensional mind, turning in anxious circles for a practical solution, but at times, in the true mind, I remembered that all my needs were taken care of, through the abundance of the Divine resources, and went out to feed the hens and get my morning egg.

One day when I came back with the small brown present, I saw a truck draw up at the plank bridge across the stream which was my link to the world. A fat old woman clambered down, with a paper in her hand. I sighed. She had come before, and there I knew went the morning for which I had other plans. Also there was nothing in the house but the egg and half a loaf of rather stale bread. But I could give her mountain tea and my attention, so I went to greet her smiling, mindful of the debt people of my pigmentation owed to people of hers.

When she was settled in the only safe chair with a mug of tea and the amenities were over, she told me why she came. She had left her job and wanted to get unemployment insurance while she looked for another, but "the people at the place" told her she couldn't have it.

"Why not, Rosella?"

"Because I quit. Have to have good reason, they said. I told them I had good reason." She frowned at me fiercely. "After while they give me the paper. So I come to you."

"What did happen?" I asked.

We finished the tea and all the bread while she told me.

She was working for a man whose unsavory reputation I knew, who ran a third-rate restaurant on the edge of the nearest town. On that particular morning she was cleaning out the ice-box when he called to her to come into the yard and shift a pile of trash. She had one more shelf to go and thought she had better finish that while the water was hot and she had her cleaning things out. Suddenly he surged into the room shouting "When I tell you to do something you get off your fat black ass and *do* it!" He struck her with the newspaper he was carrying and went out again. She thought it over for a moment, then she folded up her apron, took her things and left.

"Quite right," I said. "Did you tell them this?"

"I don't say those dirty words to nobody."

No, I thought, certainly not to a white bureaucrat.

"Did you tell them he struck you?"

"No. I just say good reason, like they told me."

"I see. Well let's fill out the form."

It took us the rest of the morning. When we came to the paragraph marked for attention, stating "applicant must furnish good and sufficient reason, etc." I wrote: "Employer used obscene and abusive language, also struck the applicant, contemptuously with a roll of newspaper." I added "applicant is personally known to me, a respected member of the community. She can produce character references. I suggest the reputation of this employer be checked, and his name be removed from the list of recommended employers in order to avoid future incidents of this kind, which may go unreported to your agency."

"Now," I said, "we'll mail this, and if they ask you to go for another interview, I'll go with you and explain to them."

She thanked me. We chatted awhile about herbs and hens, then I walked with her to the bridge, with an effort, because I was tired, and once I stumbled.

"How your legs?"

"O.K."

"You should go to the Sweat Lodge. Get help."

There was a pause.

"You believe in the Sweat Lodge?"

"Yes. In what I know of it."

"I take you some of these days."

"Fine."

I went back to the house. There on the table was a chocolate bar I had not seen her leave for me. I ate it gratefully. With the egg for supper it would see me through to my shopping day, next morning. Then I went toward the mountains. There was a tangle of willows by a stream where I sometimes went when I needed renewal. A good way to refill depletion is to lie on the earth, stretched out, head to the north. Normally I lie on my back, face to the sky. In sorrow, defeat or emergency, I lie on my stomach, face to the earth. It works. The healing currents flow. Even in cities, walled away by concrete slabs and thick cement between us and the earth, with layers of polluted air between us and the sky, the currents still flow, slower, fainter, and it may take longer to heal us, but it works. All that is needed is what is needed every time for everything, to *ask*, to set up a squawk, as Tsaviaya says, in faith and gratitude that what we ask aright is already ours.

The thoughts we emit, the words we dress them in, will naturally vary. Great Spirit, Great Imagination, Compassionate Healer, Friend of the Soul, The One Above, God, by whatever name we prefer to invoke, we thank You that all our needs are taken care of.

All our needs—spiritual, mental, emotional, physical, material, the special need of the *now*, the attack on the inner fortress of serenity which we allowed to break through our defences and affect our feelings—all of these are already taken care of. What is needed is to know this and let the knowledge seep through whatever lack we thought there was. At other times, times of no particular sharp need, the affirmation is like the warmth of the sun, steadily there to absorb for our well-being.

On this day as I lay in the healing forces a bird came to a nearby branch and sang to me for a long time with urgency in the song. It was a meadow lark, and I remembered reading somewhere that the Arapaho believe the meadow lark understands and speaks Arapaho. But I am not Arapaho, nor a meadow lark. Still I felt a gentle communion between us for which I thanked him before he flew away.

There are no meadow larks in the great cities, but even there messages of reassurance come if we have tuned in our receiving sets. I thought of friends, trapped in polluted areas, and sent them the vibrations of the pure air I was breathing, the cleansing water of the stream beside me, the sustaining strength of the earth beneath. Vibrations of thought know no barriers of time or space. They are more powerful than material conditions. Those in the cities can send them to us too, the concerts they hear, the works of art they see, the sudden sights and sounds they find significant. They do not need to send us only irritation and smog. We also have the power house of prayer, the special inter-communication of the Army of Light.

2

Ten days later the truck drew up at the bridge again and Rosella climbed down smiling. Her check had come, and she had heard of a better job to try for in a few weeks' time. She was on her way to town.

"You want a ride?"

Town was not the settlement with the general store and the service station, it was the real town with Main Street, a Safeway, a Hardware Store, fifty-eight miles away. I hesitated.

"You come. Sweat tomorrow. See Headman today."

That was different.

"Give me a moment to get changed."

"You come like that. You O.K."

My bluejeans and my shirt were old, but clean. I had washed them in the stream the day before. I looked at her. She was wearing a dress, but older Indian women had not taken to slacks. The dress was her daily wear as slacks were mine. I climbed in and we set out for the reservation.

The "Headman" we had come to see was working on his tractor at the far end of a field on the reservation. We watched him pass and repass, silhouetted against the sky, a typical country scene which I found reassuring. Presently he waved, and we got out of the car and went toward him.

"What is his name?" I asked

She hesitated.

"Eddy Strong."

Not his real name, I thought, his *white* name. Whirlpool-Strength, a massive man, huge, even for a very big Indian. I hung back while they greeted each other, smiling, joking, the Indian words crackling round them, full of old associations. Then they got down to business, the business of the white stranger she had brought with her. There was another long exchange with gestures, before he turned to me impassively.

"She say you needing help, you sick maybe."

"Yes."

"She say you want to come to Sweat Lodge?"

"I do. If you will let me."

He sighed.

"I can't say no to nobody coming for help." He said it regretfully, as though he hoped I might let him off. Part of me understood and was on his side, but more of me was stubborn.

"I do want to come."

"O.K."

He turned to Rosella.

"You tell her what she needs."

More crackling and nodding. Then he went back to his work. I thought of Robinson's "man who stood on high and faced alone the sky, whatever drove or lured or guided him."

I was feeling put down, but exultant, too, and resolute.

"Now we say hello."

Saying hello meant going to the house, the usual Government box of cinder blocks, facing us across the field. I thought how beautiful the reservation might be if Indians were encouraged to live as they used to do, in their round encampments. I remembered a painting I had seen in Fort Washakie, of seven teepees in a circle in the moonlight, each a small nest of privacy, within the protection of the whole, life in the round, in harmony with the natural rotary movement of the world.

Here there was nothing but a squat ugly shape, with everything mean about it, small mean windows, mean gray walls. It might have looked better with some semblance of a garden, a few disguising bushes, even a pathway to the door, but people forced to live in a way repugnant to them, contrary to their traditions, their ancestral ways, might see no reason to 'prettify' the approach to their condition. From what I've seen on reservations and other places where Indians live, they seem to go out of their way to strew the ground with debris and unsightliness, a form of ironic protest lost on most well-meaning white observers. But when they gather for special occasions, like the Sun Dance, and the teepees go up again in the right traditional circle, the camp is immaculate, and when they leave it every trace of anyone having been there disappears, fire holes refilled, earth raked over, not a disturbed twig, not a sign of man remains, where for days, sometimes weeks, there has been a full and active camp. It is all done without talk, without haste, in the sure and skillful way Indians use their hands on projects they approve.

The room we reached was filled with people. Blank faces turned toward us as we entered.

"I brought friend," Rosella said courageously. "She needing help."

Some of the faces cleared, some grew stonier. A woman whom I took to be the Headman's wife said politely:

"Have a chair."

I sat down in silence, smiling, I hoped not too ingratiatingly.

"Cup of coffee?"

No one else was having one. Should I accept and cause some extra trouble, or refuse and risk misunderstanding, being considered snooty, "white people set themselves up so high."

Be natural, I told myself. You're thirsty, say so.

"I'd like some coffee very much."

A girl went to get it. Conversation resumed, television chatter, artificial low-plane stuff. 'Oh,' I thought, 'if we could meet as we *are*, in our visible auras, or clothed in reassuring signs and symbols, with the certainty of understanding in our eyes! If we could know as we are known.'

In the old days, when brave met brave on the trail, there was no need for fumbling exploratory talk. Everything important was set out on their persons: family, tribe, nation, coups, exploits, likes, dislikes, triumphs, failures, revealed in the number and kind of feathers in their hair, the paint on their faces, the designs on their shirts and leggings, the number and size of fringes, the color and shape of beads and quills on their moccasins. All they had to do was to look, in silence, before they reached for tomahawk or sacred pipe.

Here *they* were looking at their inherited idea of the white oppressor, I was looking at my idea of the oppressed-but-not-by-me, and all of us were staying behind high separative walls.

I sipped and smiled and sipped, told where I lived, and what the talk was about the new cooperative, while I waited for the time to come when I could go away. It came at last. Rosella rose with "See-you's", faces visibly brightened, mine among them, as we said goodbye.

Through the shopping for offerings Rosella said that I must bring -(tobacco for the Headman, fruit juice "or cook up something" for the meal after the Sweat Lodge)- and on most of the long drive home, I thought of separateness, of individuality. Myriads of lives it took, over millions of years, to build this unique center of consciousness, this I-am-I, this small distorted viewpoint experiencing all things from the inside out. Individualization is a great and necessary step on the spiral path of evolution, but the time must come, is surely near, when separatism will give way to unity, to cooperation and fusion with the all-consciousness.

Meanwhile like deepsea divers meeting on the ocean floor we see alien, heavy, masked beings confronting us, unknown, unknowable, except for guess work and flashes of empathy, until, drawn up by our lifelines, we shuck off our heavy envelopes, and meet for the first time. . . .

Rosella stirred beside me.

"Wear old dress," she said, "old nightgown, whatever. . . .
change in house." She patted my hand, "not be afraid," and
went back to silence.

3

I had read books about the Sweat Lodge, by Indians and Whites. Theoretically I knew a good deal, but I was not prepared for the actual experience, as I stood barefooted in the long line waiting to go in. Rosella was in front of me, which was reassuring, but at the last moment she changed places with the woman ahead, and I was between two strangers. I was disconcerted, but I understood. She had stuck her neck out enough for me, now I must be on my own.

I copied what the others did, bending to pick up a handful of sage, from a mound near the entrance, brushing my hand on the earth to bless myself, stooping low to pass through the small opening, leaving all differences, all distractions and three-dimensional concerns outside the door, as I had learned to do in other holy, highly-charged places.

I followed the line, bent double beneath the low roof, to sit on a pile of fresh green tule reeds, with my legs outstretched.

There was no room to cross them, only a little space between
the soles of my feet and the central hollow where I supposed
the hot stones would be placed. It was a small lodge to hold so
many, yet everyone waiting outside got safely in, except two
men whom I could see through the doorway, tending the fire.
Both were young, but one seemed to be a "traditional" because he was wearing braids.

There was companionable laughter and murmurs in Indian
and English as we squeezed together to get settled, then a
silence. Eddy Strong rose from his seat next to the entrance,
with two forked sticks to receive the first of the stones which
the fire-tenders carried on pitchforks and put down at his feet.
He lifted them, rock by rock, and placed them at the bottom of
the pit, one for each of the four directions, one for the center.
They were red hot. Already I could feel them beginning to
scorch my feet.

Five rocks were a lot, but more were coming in. Soon the pit
was filled and still they came, until there was a pyramid of
glowing flame, scorching our faces, hands and feet. I lifted
the bunch of sage to shade my eyes, as I saw the others do,
and drew my feet beneath my gown. I put the towel round my
neck.

"Tsaviaya, may I come in?"

Eddy Strong said, "Heugh!"

Braided-man stooped to enter. We did the impossible,
squeezing closer to make room for him. The other man left the
fire and brought a bucket of water which Eddy Strong touched
to the top of the blazing pile and then put down in front of him.
The bringer crouched at the door, looking in on us.

My mind, busy with analogies, said "that's the doorman,
the outer guard, the tyler."

Suddenly I realized that I was *inside an Indian Sweat
Lodge.* Part of me feared that I did not belong there, part of me
suffered claustrophobia, part of me was scrambling up, leaping through the fire, rushing to get out—the rest of me sat still,
held down to my place, knowing it was impossible to move,
knowing that it was right for me to be there, but cold sweat
mixed with the hot sweat running from my pores.

"Everybody ready?"

There was a murmur of "Heugh's", the flap over the door

descended and the blessed privacy of darkness enveloped us. There was still a misty light from the glowing rocks, but that dimmed too as the first of the water hissed over them and a scorching blast struck me. I gasped. The woman on my right pushed my head down firmly to my knees.

"That way not so hot."

It was true. The steam flowed over my back, protected by the towel. I wondered how the men, bare to the waist, could stand it. The women at least were covered.

Her friendly hands gave me a push and pat.

"Pray. Pray *hard*. Harder you pray, less you get burned."

Voices were rising urgently. I heard the dignified woman on my left praying with heartbreak:

"Grandfather, my son is in jail, and he has sore feet."

Something inside me wept. I heard my voice join hers:

"Grandfather, her son is in jail and he has sore feet. Help him, help her, help us all . . ."

More water hissed on the rocks, another wave of steam rose over us. I cowered lower, praying harder.

I prayed to the Grandfathers and also to their helpers.

"Elementals of the fire, of the water, take us through this purification without fear, or weakness or unbearable pain. Grandfathers, I pray for all of these . . . help us . . . I pray. . . ."

A tremendous nasal chant broke out, covering our voices as the searing steam covered our bodies, washing mind, heart, spirit. The sound was new to me, alien, strange, and yet familiar too. I knew these ancient single syllables. I even understood what they meant. Sometimes, somewhere, in vanished Atlantis, perhaps, I sat "in a sacred manner", emitting sounds like these.

The chant went on and on and on. The steam went on and on and on. My human overcoat grew weak, my senses were failing. Eddy Strong said "Heugh!". The doorflap opened. Light and air rushed in. Someone said "Open the back please." Another flap went up.

"Keep low, you fellows."

The steam cleared. I sat up cautiously. Some were crouching forward, some lay against the sides, a few, sitting up, were looking down or had their eyes closed. Everyone seemed limp, exhausted.

"Tsaviaya, paiha."

Eddy Strong passed a dipperful of water from the bucket in front of him to the one who spoke.

"Tsaviaya, water please."

Again the dipper went round the lodge to the asking one.

"Tsaviaya, may I go out?"

"Heugh!"

An old man got up. Though he sat near the door he travelled the entire circle, treading on several feet, before he reached it. So, everything went clockwise. *Paiha* meant water: Tsaviaya must be Eddy Strong's real name. It was possible to go out when the flaps were open, a thought I had better push away.

I would have liked to ask for *paiha* too, but the woman next to me did not, so I sat still, *thinking* water to refresh me, and it did. Thirst grew bearable, then went away. Those who had stepped outside came back, the flap was lowered, the praying began. This was the second round, differing from the first, not only in the new rhythm and the words of the song, but in the feel of things. It was as though we had invoked the spirits in the first round, implored their help, asked for their compassion; now we were greeting them, relieved that they had come to bless us. Shouts went up, sounding through the song. Here and there people stopped singing to pray, as though we must restate the urgencies afflicting us, the needs for which we had asked the Spirits to come in.

The rocks were blackened now, the darkness complete, the steam more penetrating. Again the neighbor pushed my head down, and I found myself gasping and choking, as I tried to sing the familiar chant, the familiar words, and underneath them 'Help us! Help us! Help! It ended at last, when it seemed that another second of steam would disintegrate endurance.

"Bless yourselves!"

There was the sound of patting and grunting. Hands patted my head, my chest, then I patted myself, and found that I was grunting gutturally, too.

"Heugh!"

The flap flew up, the air rushed in. No need to tell us this time to keep down, we were all bowed forward, some of the men on hands and knees, heads to the ground in front of the fire, others leaning backward or sideways. Some were lying down behind their neighbors, who had hunched forward to give them room. "Greater love hath no man, than this," I thought, "to go nearer to that fire for another's sake!" Slowly we recovered enough to sit up.

Now that the rocks were darker I could look at them without burning my eyeballs. I saw that most of them had 'faces,'— grinning, frowning, grimacing, expressively alive. There was one big rock in front of me with a particularly knowing look, friendly enough, but sardonic, amused to find me there.

I looked above it, to the eyes of the man sitting opposite Tsaviaya, and received a vibratory shock, a wave of power. This was a Personage, small, slight, with a differently shaped face from the others, a man from another tribe perhaps. I looked down, conscious that I had stared at him, that he knew what I was thinking and a lot more. The Singer sat next to him, the man who led the chants. Probably the three or four men and women nearest Tsaviaya had special functions in the lodge.

"Paiha!" the Singer said. The dipperful was passed to him. Several more asked and received it. I wanted water badly, but none of the women spoke, perhaps women weren't entitled to it. As I hesitated, a friendly nudge and whisper urged "ask." So I said "Paiha, please", and the dipperful was passed to me. I copied what I had watched the others do, raising it first to Those Above, pouring a little to Mother Earth, before I drank, bathed my face and emptied the rest over my head. I returned the dipper gratefully. The water was blessed, full of cool, healing power. It came from a mountain stream, or deep protected well, and tasted as water used to taste.

I sat back, refreshed, and almost ready for the third round to begin. Again the relief of darkness, the prayers, the rising steam, the high nasal chanting in new rhythm. Again my voice rose with the rest and I seemed to understand the meaning of the syllables.

This time I felt some mighty, attentive Being stood on the

burning rocks, slowly scrutinizing each of us as it rotated. I was aware of force flowing over us. My neighbor gasped, she cried out beneath the chanting. It had new rhythm now, no longer imploring, no longer urgent, more a receiving song for these healing streaming rays.

My turn came. I could feel the burning power like a blow upon the solar plexus, then a pause as though It waited for response. This was not a one-way operation, I was meant to do my part, to ask for help, but all I found to say was "Grandfather, thank you, I thank you!"

A slow withdrawal began, back to the center of the fire, back to the Being standing on it, taking away everything released, as an undercurrent drags sand, pebbles, seaweed to the sea. The focus of attention moved on, my neighbors rejoined the chanting, I too sang.

When all had been surveyed and treated, when the circle was complete, the singing stopped. Tsaviaya said "Bless yourselves!" Pattings and murmurings began, the last water soaked the stones, the cloud of steam drenched us.

"Heugh!" The flap opened, the steam rushed out, light and air came in. Someone said "Open the back, please!" The back flap went up. We were lying in heaps, whatever ways we could, and so we stayed until Tsaviaya said "Last round! Clear up in front of you."

People took pieces of the tule reeds beneath them and began to scrape the ground between the rocks and their feet. I did the same, smoothing down the earth. No water was offered. The flaps closed, the fourth round began.

The singing was different, stately, slow, rhythmic, like the beating of great wings. Suddenly I realized there *was* the beating of great wings. I felt, I knew, I saw behind my eyelids, Grandfather Eagle circling above us, preparing to depart. The singing changed, the rhythm changed, reaching upward in awe, in sorrow of farewell. I saw the great black wings grow white, grow gold, like the sails of a clipper in the sunset. They dwindled, they diminished. The song died.

Tsaviaya said in a small voice, "Bless yourselves." But how could any blessing be added to the blessing already given?

"Heugh!" The flaps went up for the last time. We straightened ourselves, for now the Pipe was coming in. The doorman knelt to present it, the man opposite Tsaviaya lit it for the doorman to smoke, received it again, smoked it and sent it on its clockwise way. Each took it from his neighbor, each performed the same rite, lowering it to touch the ground, raising it to smoke, sometimes over the smoker's body, sometimes released into the air.

It was a long, slow process. As I waited for my turn I tried to remember what I knew about the Pipe. It was the central, most sacred object of the Indian way of life, the essential channel - pipeline - between the Great Spirit and His children. Words I had read came to me clearly, without effort, as everything came in the Sweat Lodge.

"Behold this pipe! Always remember how sacred it is, and treat it as such, for it will take you to the end. With this pipe the two-legged will increase, and there will come to them all that is good. From above Wakan-tanka has given you this sacred pipe, so that through it you may have knowledge."

That was the Sacred Buffalo Woman of the Lakota Sioux.

"O Wakan-Tanka, You are the truth. The two-legged peoples who put their mouths to this pipe will become the truth itself; there will be in them nothing impure. Help us to walk the sacred path of life without difficulty, with our minds and hearts continually fixed on You."

That was High Hollow Horn.

"With this sacred Pipe you will walk upon the Earth, for the Earth is sacred. Every step taken upon her should be a prayer. The bowl of this Pipe is of red stone. It is of the Earth. The stem of this Pipe is of wood, and this represents all that grows upon the Earth."

That was why we touched it to the ground.

"The feathers which hang where the stem fits into the bowl represent the Eagle and all the wingeds of the air. All things of the universe are joined to you who smoke the Pipe, all send their voices to the Great Spirit. When you pray with this Pipe, you pray for and with everything created."

That was the Sacred White Buffalo Woman. I remembered where I had first read it, on a bulletin a friend sent to me from the National Monument at Pipestone, in Minnesota, where for thousands of years Indians of every tribe quarried the sacred stone for their pipeheads, and still do. The stone for this one must have come from there.

Now it was drawing nearer. My neighbor rubbed her hands on the ground and then together. I did the same, to receive it in the ancient way. At last it was passed to me, I held it in my hands, feeling the stem, smooth, cool, charged with powerful vibrations, lowering the head to Mother Earth, blowing the puffs that went out strongly, up to the Great Spirit, down to Mother Earth, toward the Four Directions, then the puffs for what I should be asking, healing for my human overcoat, but again all I thought of was "I thank You." I passed it on, and sat back relieved, released from anxiety that I would fail, that it would go out and have to be relit, or even that I would drop it. Pipestone is easily broken.

I had given up smoking years before and developed a strong distaste for anything to do with it, but this smoking was different. The tobacco was sweet and gentle, not like other tobacco, Kinikinik perhaps, grown organically and smudged with sage. There was no feather on the Pipe, but one dangled from the roof, and there was something above Tsaviaya's head that looked like an eagle's wing. It came to me that the hole in the center of the lodge was the bowl of a Pipe, that the lodge itself was a Pipe, that we were grains of tobacco in the Great Spirit's Pipe. A surge of joy shook me. I wanted to cry "I love you!" to everyone in the circle, but they were deep in meditation, gone 'behind the blanket' to their secret communions as I should go to mine.

The Pipe reached Tsaviaya. He held it up, turning it slowly round, then followed the ritual way, smoking what remained. It was a long smoke, spiralling through the lodge, to this one, to that one, to me, filling our nostrils with sweetness.

Suddenly there was a stir. Tsaviaya handed the Pipe to the doorman, who placed it on the mound outside, then he took up his bunch of sage, his towel, and stooping low, went out, followed by all of us in order. It seemed strange to stand erect in the sunshine of what was still the same afternoon, apparently. Time was not, in the Sweat Lodge. If we had emerged at midnight or dawn of another day it would not have surprised me.

4

After the high experience, the corresponding slump. The distractions and hindrances I had left at the door of the lodge rejoined me, powerfully. I would have liked to crawl beneath a secluded tree, lie down on my back and slowly, gently recover. Then I would have liked to drive off by myself, up a mountain road, to give appropriate offerings and thanks to the Grandfathers. Instead I, a loner, uneasy in any group, even a group of familiar friends, must strip off my sodden covering and dress in front of these curious, even hostile strangers, for so they seemed to have become, inspite of empathy and closeness in the Sweat Lodge.

The noise of strident voices in Indian and English hurt my ears, still quivering to the beauty of the chants. I supposed it was a let-down, a relief for them, and wished it might be so for me, but mindless chatter, like T.V. commercials, compulsive giggling, this sort of vibration, seemed on a strangely low

level for people who had just been purified to smoke the
sacred Pipe together.

I was expecting wise, gentle comment on the shared experience, or sensitive silence, not these down to earth raucous
exchanges, and not the earth of the Planetary Spirit, the De-
vas, the Nature Elementals. I wanted to leave, hugging the
shreds of the high experience, but I knew that I must stay.
Eating together after the Sweat Lodge was an important part
of the ritual.

We joined the men in the living room, a long, narrow, out-
of-proportioned oblong with concrete walls, and high small
windows, bare of furniture, except for a trestle table in the
middle. There were no chairs, we sat on the floor with our
backs to the walls. Some of the men were busy putting out
food, others joined their families. The joking and the laughter
increased, with a sexual tinge to it, the sort of stale bawdy
jokes some adolescents enjoy, before they discover passion,
real passion, not the Kinsey kind, and sex becomes important
and private. As someone has said, 'only the chaste are passionate. What have the promiscuous to be passionate about?'

This joking, this exchange of personal sexual insults, was
not intended to be crude. It was the harmless show-off of the
uninvolved. It reminded me of devout Catholic friends who
liked to tell off-color stories about the Virgin Mary, but would
have resented it if I had. It was a way of saying she belonged
to them. It was a sort of frank enjoyment, a happy acceptance
among sure friends of the male-female complementary roles,
important in tribal societies. There was also another factor, a
drawing together of the group to shut out intruders. I thought
of Johnson's remark to Boswell and some friends, when they
were walking down the street, laughing. "Sirs, let us be
grave. Here comes a fool."

Those who found ribaldry disturbing had something wrong
with them, were fools or intruders. At least the group did not
bother to be "grave" in front of me. That was something. Still,
the timing jarred me, and I was glad when Tsaviaya put an
end to talk. He came to the head of the table and held up a
huge hand. Silence, like the darkness in the Sweat Lodge,
obliterated lesser preoccupations. We bowed our heads, and

the grace began. It was in Indian, then in English. At the end of it he welcomed the one I thought of as "Power Man", by a name I didn't catch, "our brother, who has come a long way from his own Sweat to be with us here, and will come back some of these days to help us." Then he said "doorman first."

A line formed behind the "bringer" who had guarded the flaps. I waited till most of the people were coming back with plates and mugs full of delicious smelling food. Then I went up in turn, suddenly very hungry. "Take a little of everything," seemed to be the rule. There was acorn soup, pi-nut mush, Indian fried bread, a "gravy" of berries and flour, the usual potluck collection of casseroles, salads, fruits, cakes, juices, coffee. I gathered that it was important to take things in the order they were placed, and that the first four dishes were essential. After helping ourselves to those, we could choose among the rest, but it was safer, more polite, to sample everything. The grace had stressed "bless this food and bless the hands that prepared it." No hands should be slighted.

I was conscious that everything I did was being carefully observed. I represented—I was hoping I could alter—a stereotyped image of "the whites", instead of one human being who had come there in good will; and only, but this they might not believe, a small segment of the most ignorant whites. How absurd racial prejudices were in the Atomic-Aquarian Age! Must minorities, when they emerge into power, repeat the worst mistakes of the majorities? Who could be sure of ethnic purity? In the United States the melting pot has been melting vigorously for two hundred years. Before that, in Europe, Asia, everywhere, races were blending. Moreover was ethnic purity still part of the Plan? Weren't we supposed to move forward to a more universal, comprehensive human condition?

I pondered while I ate, smiling at this one, that one, tentatively, getting no real response. Rosella went by among the early leavers. She paused to say "you made it. See you." My friend in the Sweat Lodge also paused to smile at me encouragingly. I felt her smile was real. "So you alright." I said "yes, thanks to you." After awhile I felt I too could leave, neither in the first nor the last group, but unobtrusively in the middle. I said a general goodbye at the door with the others.

There were answering "see-you's" and I slipped outside, into the cool, blessed darkness underneath the stars.

During the long drive home and in the weeks that followed, I went through the experience of the Sweat Lodge, recalling, analysing, absorbing it slowly, as one distills the essence of high moments. First I thought of this–plane reactions, of how interesting and inspiriting it was that in 1965 Sweat Lodges were beginning to return to the land from which they had been obliterated. They were being rebuilt from memories and impressions of those elders who had sweated in them as children, from records and photographs preserved in such places as the Smithsonian, from oral traditions remembered and handed on to those who could listen, but most efficaciously through dreams and visions from the Grandfathers.

The climate of ignorance and prejudice was changing a little in the white world, toward curiosity, respect, and a belated wish to preserve some at least of the traditional Indian way. Books were beginning to appear, such as John Neihardt's *Black Elk Speaks*, Frank Waters' *Book of the Hopi*, and Joseph Epes Brown's *The Sacred Pipe*. There were also the Ernest Thompson Seton books of my childhood, and later his Gospel of the Red Man, but until lately these were not revered and pressed upon the educated young as classics on the lists of required reading for college courses, yet how pertinent they were to the growth of understanding, the expansion of consciousness, the quest for Cosmic Reality, in other words, the pursuit of happiness, also enjoined upon the young.

All that had come down to those inhabiting this Turtle Island after the suppression, were footnotes by specialists, distorted accounts by early missionaries and explorers, the often misguided, misinterpreted "findings," of archeologists and biased historians, with here and there stray phrases thoughtlessly used in daily talk.

"If you want something you must sweat for it."

"Put that in your pipe and smoke it."

I had a library of Indian books and much theoretical knowledge of Medicine Men and rituals, but my one experience of a Sweat Lodge, changed what I thought I knew.

There was first the total involvement of spirit, mind, *and body*. I had prayed *and sweated*, for a stranger in prison, for sick people, for myself, for the whole brave human race. It was sacrifice and sharing in a more basic way than kneeling in a church had brought to me.

Sharing was the point. Someone gathered and brought the tule reeds. Someone brought the rocks and the wood for the fire. Someone drew the water and carried it in pails. Many hands must have built the Sweat Lodge, cutting and trimming the willow trees, planting them in the ground, bending them symmetrically together to support the roof. In the old days someone would have cured the deerskin or the buffalo hide to stretch on the framework. Then there would be a ritual to bless it, in which everyone concerned would take part.

The description of such a ritual was in Chapter III of Brown's *The Sacred Pipe*. There was a diagram showing the Inipi, the purification lodge. The Sweat Lodge here was made by another tribe, but the principle was the same.

I thought of the circle, in all its symbolism, from a glyph of the Creator, that Point within the Circle, whose center is everywhere, to its representative, the sun, source of light, life and spiritual illumination. From there I went to meditation on the Medicine Wheel, a mandala of concentric depths and intricate designs, where everything in the universe has its appropriate place.

Dante's summary of his vision, in the last three lines of the *Paradise*, sings:

The Will rolled onward, like a wheel
in even motion by the Love impelled,
  that moves the sun in Heaven and all the stars.

The sixteenth-century mystic, Jacob Boehme, wrote in his *Confession*: "The Being of God is like a Wheel, wherein many wheels are made in one another, upwards, downwards, crossways, and yet continually turn all of them together. At which indeed, when a man beholds the wheel, he highly marvels."

The mandala of the Medicine Wheel represents the sun, the earth, the sky, the water and the four winds. On that level it stands for the creation of the world, but it can also stand for the progression of a single day, from sunrise to sunset, and the night to follow, as it can represent the circle of human life from birth to death and the spirit road beyond.

There is also the natural rotary movement of the world. All things are circular. The sun is round, the bird's nest is round, life is a round between birth and death, everything revolves in its appointed place on the Wheel of the Universe. People thrive best when they are in harmony with their surroundings and their surroundings mirror universal law. Buckminster Fuller's geodesic dome is no new concept. The well-being it induces was basic to the Indian way of life. The secrets of the Circle became second nature to those who followed the way of the wheel.

Tsaviaya's Sweat Lodge was round, with the opening to the East. The hollow in the center to receive the heated rocks was round, representing the hub of the Wheel, or in some traditions, the navel of Mother Earth. We, sitting on the tule reeds in our tight circle, represented the interdependence of the created and our relationship with the Creator.

I thought about these things and decided to practice living in the round as the best way of absorbing the essence of the Sweat Lodge. Not the round of the hymn, "The daily round, the common task,/Will furnish all we need to ask", though that was true too, and not the dreary drudgery I thought it meant, when I heard it in church. The daily round could be an enchanted ring. But the round I was thinking of, the round I wanted to practice, was my place in the great wheeling dance of the Universe, where all things move inward from the circumference to the Center.

I went to the round horse trough behind the house, hidden by willows, wild rose bushes and sage, filled from the mountain stream running in through a hose, running out through another. Here I usually took three dips a day, at sunrise, high noon and sunset. Now I added more to the simple ritual of purification and praise. I stood in the center of a wheel of water, sun-quickened but still cold from the melting snow at its source. I raised my hands to the sky, I turned to the four directions, asking that the healing, cleansing power of the water should flow through every cell and atom of my being, I immersed myself in turn to the east, the south, the west, the north, then I sent the essence of the water out into the world, from the hub where I stood, along the paths to the four directions, to the hot, the angry, the fevered, all who could be reached through this water for blessing.

It is a simple sacrament. Those who do not have round horsetroughs or secluded swimming holes, can do it in the shower. The shower ring is usually a circle and so can be transformed to a mandala, with four radii. The water should be blessed from the first drops, Such is the power of the Grandfathers, that even chlorinated, heavily polluted water will be purified to cleanse us from more than physical dirt, then sprayed from the circumference to the parched, exhausted, longing world. In this way, every time we bathe, we can help ourselves, and also help to restore the four kingdoms, mineral, vegetable, animal, human, all our planet earth, to joy and radiant health. We are not helpless, we have infinite power, *now*, to draw on.

There are circles, great mandalas everywhere, waiting to be recognized and used.

5

A few days later I ran into my friend of the Sweat Lodge. We stood on the street corner exchanging how-are-you's.

"Sermons", she said beaming. "Start tomorrow. You come."

It was neither an invitation nor a question, it was a statement. I temporized.

"Where?"

"In the Sermon House."

One of the many missions, I supposed a little sadly. Apart from the divisive effect upon community life of so many competing sects and churches, most of the ministers and leaders implied and some openly taught that the ancient ways of worshipping the Great Spirit were heathen superstitions, the Medicine Man an evil witchdoctor in league with Satan, the Sweat Lodge an open door to Hell.

Her church might be different, one of the more tolerant, since she attended Sweats. Because I wanted her to go on talking, I asked:

"When?"

The smile faded. Pinned down to time she turned evasive as Indians do, with expressions of surprised distaste for something gross or indiscreet, then the almost imperceptible shrug, the recovery, the effort to explain the obvious to the ignorant.

"When the time is right." She made helpful motions. "Sun go down."

An evening service. A series of services. She had said 'sermons', she had said 'start'. I searched for some plausible excuse. Then what she was saying hit me. *Ceremonies*, in the *Ceremony* House. That would be near the Sweat Lodge.

"I'll be there."

She nodded. "Bring cushion. Dish of food. I see you."

She turned away. The light for my crossing changed. *Walk* the sign said. I walked, but in my heart I was dancing. I had gone the four rounds of the Sweat Lodge, I had smoked the Pipe, I was accepted. No Indian Sermony should be totally strange to me. It would be another deep experience.

Next day I went what I thought would be early to the reservation and found that I was almost late. There were cars and trucks in the field and a line of people outside the tipi of the visiting Medicine Man. I recognized several faces. No one seemed surprised to see me, but no one spoke and no one smiled. This was a serious line-up. One by one they were entering the tipi and after what seemed a long wait, coming out again, still in silence, scattering to their cars. Presently I saw them with bundles—'cushion, dish of food'—making towards the Strongs' house at the far end of the field.

I was last in the line, 'tail end of the cow', but when my turn came it seemed too soon. I would have liked to wait a little longer taking in the scene. It must have looked like this a hundred, two hundred, ageless years ago. There was nothing of the twentieth century here but the cars and trucks behind me. Looking forward all I saw was the tipi with its cluster of tall poles against the sky, an Arapaho tipi, that much I knew. The visiting doctor was an Arapaho Buffalo Man.

His shelter came with him on his truck. In the old days the poles would have been attached to horses, and before the horses came, to dogs or women, dragging everything needed for nomadic life. In the evenings the poles supported the tipis. What could be more convenient? If the Indian, scorned for "not discovering the wheel" had bothered to use it for transport he could not have gone where he needed to go, nor would the wheels have been useful when he arrived. Wheels were heavy clumsy things, needing constant repair, and roads to travel on. Poles could be easily replaced and could go anywhere a horse, or a dog, or a woman could drag them.

Wheels were important only for the concepts they embodied. Native Americans had the Great Medicine Wheel. They lived their lives in the round and knew the symbolic meaning of the wheel in all its forms. Circles and discs were significant, so also squares and poles. I counted nine poles on the tipi. Numbers mattered. In the old days it would have taken eighteen to twenty skins for the covering of a tipi, perhaps more for a Medicine Man's lodge, and it would have been decorated in vivid traditional patterns.

The tipi ahead of me was made of canvas, with no decorations. Still it was the right shape and size and there was an authentic and powerful Medicine Man inside it, as I knew from my experience in the Sweat Lodge, for this was the "Power Man" as I thought of him.

Almost too quickly my turn came to push aside the flap and stoop to enter. (Bow your head, indeed one must, and compress oneself as well). When I stood up I was surprised by the cool spaciousness and eased into well-being by the lack of clutter.

Power Man sat on a low couch covered by a blanket of turquoise blue marked with designs. He did not greet me or look up. His wife was sitting on the ground beside him working on something in front of her. She smiled and beckoned to me to come nearer. I saw that she was filling small squares of white material with pinches of tobacco and tying them together. She put them down to take up her husband's pipe.

"You want to present the pipe?"

She showed me how to fill it, how to hold it, and told me what to say when I presented it.

"Then you tell him what you want."

Seeing me hesitate she added "you are ill? You have trouble? Family need help? You tell him. Only thing you can't ask is money. You can ask for job you need to take care of your family and all like that, but not money. The Grandfathers don't hear money"

She motioned me toward Power Man and I went, carrying the Pipe, trembling a little, taken aback. What *did* I want? I was ill, I was broke, I had plenty of trouble, but I had not come there for that, nor for cheap curiosity. I was curious, eager, yes, but I had come, I thought, with a confused idea of offering myself in service, in belated reparation for injustices done to the redskinned peoples.

In the few steps it took to reach him I understood that an offer of this kind would be a reversal of the situation as they saw it, perhaps a reversal of reality. I had nothing that these wanted or needed or would accept. The power to bless, to heal, to enlighten belonged to *them*. I was there to receive, to be the suppliant taker, the "beholden" one.

I said the words she had told me, I presented the Pipe and then I stood expectantly before him. There was a pause. He looked at me, looked into me, looked beyond me. I gazed back in trust, but I could not speak. He began to smoke the tobacco I had packed for him, while I stood, head bowed, offering myself, asking silently that I might become a bridge between 'the blessed company of all faithful people' under any color of skin, all faithful creatures, including birds and animals and growing things, and that, in time, I might become an instrument of the Great Spirit, a healer of miseries.

The smoke curled between us, travelling round my head. Presently it was gone. He looked up at me. "The Grandfathers know what you want. They hear what you say. You get your answer. May not come quick, all at once. You get it when the time is right."

He gave me the Pipe and I took it back to his wife, who said "tomorrow when you come bring_____" she told me what, how much, and smiled dismissal.

I lifted the flap and bowed myself out. More people were waiting who had arrived while I was in the timeless time inside. Still shaking a little I walked with an effort to the car, gathered up the cushion and the dish of fruit, and went on the next lap of this path on which, without premeditation or enough conscious thought, I had suddenly set my feet.

6

Once more I was in the Strong's living room. I had wondered why it was so disproportionately planned, so large, so oblong, so bare of furniture. Now I began to understand. Even the table where we had eaten after the Sweat Lodge was gone. There were only people, seated against the walls, or waiting to be placed. I joined a huddle near the door. A man took my dish of fruit away and put it in the kitchen where I could see a trestle heaped with food.

Tsaviaya was standing in the center, checking a list. As he called their names, people went forward, clutching their cushions, to be seated. The man who had taken my dish went over to him and said something. They both looked at me. Tsaviaya beckoned.

"You being doctored?"

"I think so."

He shook his head at such a foolish answer.

44

"You presented your Pipe?"

"Yes."

He wrote my name on his list, ticked it off and showed me where to sit, in the front row between a young woman and an older man. I was glad to take my allotted place and become less obtrusive. Mine was the only non-Indian face in all that gathering. I thought there must be well over a hundred people, men, women, children, babies, all on cushions on the floor, each with a right to the same amount of space, each equally important, in true Democracy. I watched them being seated, some in families, some alone like me. Soon we formed two lines along the three sides of the room. The fourth side, facing mine, was empty. I saw my friend of the Sweat Lodge, and others whom I knew and tentatively smiled at them, but there was no answering smile, no flicker of recognition. It was not a social occasion. We were together but alone.

There was no talking. When everyone was seated there was a long pause, a time of preparation. I grew conscious of scrutinizing glances and then I remembered another time and place when I had felt as I was feeling now, self-consciously aware that my human envelope marked me out of place, though then as now I knew that I was where I had wanted to be and where I should be.

It was in Paris, in nineteen twenty seven, or twenty eight, in the Cathedral of Notre Dame. I had gone there on a weekday morning to rest and meditate. There was a shadowed corner that I always chose, against a pillar, from where I could see the great Rose window, one of the world's most intricate mandalas, charged with force and light. The organ was playing but I was alone in the dim vastness of the nave.

Suddenly the great doors in the west were flung open. I had never seen this before. Always one entered by a smaller door cut in a panel. Flags were coming in, the Fleur de Lys, the Tricolor, others with numbers and devices. Behind them a procession in dark civilian suits marched towards the nave. As they drew nearer I saw that they were all young men, most of them adolescents. The lettering on their banners said J.O.C. Jeunes Ouvriers Catholiques. These were the Jocistes, young Catholic workmen of France coming to their cathedral

for a special service. And here was I, not Catholic, not a
workman, not French, infiltrated among them with no way of
escape. Fortunately I was in a dark suit too, and hatless and
shorthaired. At a distance I might pass, until I had to stand,
and then the skirt would give me away, and brand me as a
member of the other sex. I shrank against my pillar nervously,
as the row of young workers filed in beside me.

The lights went on, the organ blared triumphantly, the choir
stalls were filling with white robes. Another procession was
forming in the chancel. Cross, candles, incense, acolytes,
priests, and behind them that rarely seen Prince of the
Church, the Archbishop of Paris, in all his glittering vest-
ments, escorted by two lesser luminaries in theirs. We
kneeled to receive his blessing as he passed. When we rearranged ourselves the boy beside me gave me a quick
glance, and held out his manual for us to share. He had the
pinched face, Pierrot-qui-rit, Pierot-qui-pleure, of the Paris
poor. He should have been in his beret and black tablier,
lugging his books to school. He looked about fourteen, but he
must have been older, beyond the legal age for leaving
school, and he was now officially a Jociste and a man.

We followed the service together, companionably, praying,
singing, taking the Archbishop's address to heart. By the time
the procession reformed and the great church emptied, I was
completely at ease as a young Catholic worker. Later I wondered sadly what became of him and those two thousand or so
young men of France when World War Two overwhelmed the
world.

The woman on my left stirred. Her stirring brought me rushing through decades of years onto my cushion beside her. As
she lifted herself a little to ease her legs, I became aware of
the cramp in my own legs and the pain in my back. I was badly
out of condition to sit cross-legged and keep still for any
length of time. I began to envy the line of early comers behind
us with the wall to lean against, although sitting in the front
row we would perhaps see more.

But now there was another sort of stir at the door. A Prince of
this Church was coming in, the Medicine Man, in his regalia
of sweat shirt, blue jeans, and dignity, followed by his wife

and four men. They took their places against the empty side of
the room facing me. I took advantage of the general con-
vergence of attention upon them to shift my weight to a different set of aches and settle myself more sternly to endure
discomfort.

The ceiling lights went on, two naked bulbs dangling from
their cords. Men were nailing blankets over the doors and
windows. A comfortable sense of being separated from the
outside world set in. I had felt this in the Sweat Lodge, and
also the obliteration of watch-clock time.

Power Man sat still beside his wife. Now and then she
murmured something to him and he smiled. He had a sweet,
gentle smile. The four men with him were making preparations in the center of the room. They were marking off a
long oblong, putting colored cloths on sticks at each corner,
joining them with strips of white. I thought, though I could not
be sure, that these were the little bundles I had seen Power
Man's wife making in the tipi. If so, she must have worked for
many hours, because the oblong was about thirty feet by
twenty. Its shape reminded me of pictures I had seen of Long-
houses, and also the arrangement of a Masonic Temple. I was
familiar with the concept of the Guardian Wall surrounding
highly charged places where power would be generated.
Sometimes it was permanently built into the floor, here it was
being formed in front of us for everyone to see but not to touch.
No one could leave his place to reach out blundering hand or
foot to desecrate or interfere with this wall and the sacred
things it would enclose, yet all could watch the preparations
step by step and ponder them.

I knew that I would enter more completely into the mysteries
of the coming ceremony if I related what I saw and heard to
other experiences and traditions, so that I might be drawn in
from the start and especially that I might not, deceived by the
casual-seeming way things seemed to be happening, miss
some inner significance and be left on the outer rim of the
unaware.

Everything did seem to be done casually, in a leisurely,
even haphazard way by *Tsaviaya* and these other heavy
thickset men stepping lightly in their shoeless feet, no bustle,

no brisk movement, no acolyte self-importance, no bobbing, no tinkling of bells.

I thought of the many times I had taken off my shoes, in India before entering a temple or a shrine, and lately in the Sweat Lodge. I thought of Moses and the Voice from the Burning Bush: "Put off thy shoes from off thy feet, for the place whereon thou standest is holy ground."

Now three of the men started round the room carrying a bucket of water, a dish of burning herbs and a tray heaped with something else. The man with the bucket raised it to the lips of each one in the back line first and then the front. The man beside me steadied the bucket with his hands. I copied his example. It was pure mountain water, cold and invigorating. This must be the equivalent of the Asperges, but instead of sprinkling the building, which was already consecrated, judging from the vibrations sweeping through it, we were drinking the consecrated water to purify and steady ourselves, and coming from the startle of the everyday world we needed it.

Here came the dish of burning herbs which would be the Censing. "In every place incense shall be offered," in every place, this place too. Native Americans come nearer to observing this precept than those who sing it once a week in churches. They use it not only in sweats, and ceremonies, and sacred dances, they "smudge" themselves, their children, their houses, their trucks, their food, every object given to them, everything they give away, and naturally their Sweat Lodges, Ceremony Houses and their sacred Pipes.

"As this incense rises . . . let Thy Holy Angels . . ." the spirits of the earth and the water and the air and the fire, the winged ones, the messengers, the eagles, Grandfather Eagle, mediator between creatures and the Great Imagination Which created them, "encompass Thy people and breathe forth upon them the spirit of Thy blessing."

Copying my neighbor again, I took smoke in my hands, wafted it over my face and head and the sides of my body down to my feet, said "thank you" to the server and bowed my head.

Now came the tray filled with sprigs of sage. Each took one and put it behind the right ear, bowed, said "thank you", in

English which seemed strange until I remembered that the Indians present came from different tribes and did not know each other's tongues, some of them knew no Indian. English had to be the unitive language.

Now we were all properly prepared, down to the smallest baby, but what was the significance of the sprig of sage behind the ear? The Bible and other sacred texts were full of references to ears, singular and plural. I must look them up. Probably the most relevant was "He that hath an ear to hear, let him hear."

Sage I knew, and some of the uses it could be put to, perhaps among its other properties it was also an ear opener. When I got home I would study the ear, the spiral shell, the vibrations and mechanism of communicated sound, and reflect on the inner and outer hearing.

Meanwhile Power Man had taken off his shoes and was standing in the middle of the oblong with his back to the east. Two men tied his hands behind his back, took the cord down to his feet and fastened them securely. Then they wrapped him in the blue blanket I had seen in the tipi. Its design was apparent to me now. It was a great Thunderbird in black and white. They roped it round him, pulled it over his head, tied it round the neck, laced it to his sides, so that he looked like a tall, gaunt Egyptian mummy, supported by attendants. They lowered him in one swift movement (after all the slow ones) face to the floor. Tsaviaya circled him three times waving a burning "punk" of sweet grass.

Then the lights went out. This was startling and unexpected. It was also a growing relief. Gone were the rows of faces, the feeling of fending off stares, the need to focus attention on what was happening. I had thought the blanketing-off of doors and windows was a symbol of protection, of shutting out the world; instead it was the shutting in of night, the primordial darkness, out of which all things emerge.

I remembered a stage in the Mysteries where it was said that the light of that degree was "but darkness visible", an anticipatory state, an expansion of consciousness through the controlled suppression of a physical sense. I sat still on my cushion. My back no longer hurt. There was about me nothing but the soothing silence of the black abyss.

Then the drums began.

7

I have heard drums in many places, in Africa at night—but not in total darkness, there were torches, there was moonlight—at funerals and military parades, for sorrow, for pride, for incitement to war; in classical music in concert halls; in the infernal din of "rock" on the radio before one could leap to turn it off. I understood the effect of rhythmic sound upon the human envelope, but I had never heard *drumming* before, never the rhythm, the urgency, the overwhelming summons, rushing upon me now.

I swayed in ecstasy, the sage quivered behind my ear. Sage must be for protection, because this thunder breaking over us was almost beyond the edge of bearing. In Africa I learned that drums in the hands of Shamans and Medicine Men can induce a state of ecstasy. Ecstasy and terror are only a sway apart. I was told that the drum represents the heart and also the sacrificial altar; that it stands for the relationship between the upper and lower spheres; it is thunder and lighting. "Out of the darkness came primordial sound", first of all things to be created, cause of the birth of the world.

In the beginning was the stupendous, detonating WORD.

Yes, yes, to all of these, but still I had not heard the totality of *sound* until the Cry began, drumming and voices soaring together, imploring Those Above to enter and take the places prepared for Them. I understood what we were doing, I knew the urgency, the meaning of the Cry, and with those around me I began to cry too, in the high nasal tones of a voice I did not recognize, yet it was coming through my lips, and the modulations of sound and the ancient syllables were familiar to me.

This was the Invocation, the Come-in-Song to the Spirits, and a summons to us to be ready to receive Them when They came.

It was a night of contrasts. I had been blinded and soothed by darkness, deafened and exalted by sound, now I was dropped into silence, fathomless, complete. Everything had stopped. After a pause the gentle voice of Power Man's wife said with authority: "The first group in the front line stand up." There was a movement at the far end of the line, but no one near me stirred, so I sat still, The quiet voice continued: "Is everyone up and ready?" Someone said "Yes". The drumming and the chanting began again, but it was different this time, not an agonized cry for help, more a firm commitment, a let-it-be-so force.

Lights began to flicker about us like those seen in seances. I could hear the rattling of gourds, mingled with the drumming, buried beneath the singing, sounding in the pauses. Again there was silence.

"You may sit down," said the voice. "Next group stand up please."

It was still not my group, but the flickering lights were nearer and the clicking sounds. Now and then there seemed to be some indistinct movement beneath the sparks. The chant changed to an easier one. I sang with the others. When a child cried out or a baby wailed, we sang louder.

Then it all stopped again. The voice said: "You may sit down. Next group stand up please." Now it was my turn. I

stumbled up awkwardly, keeping my heels against the cushion to be sure that I was facing the right way. The woman
beside me grasped my hand to pull us into better position,
gave it a little comforting squeeze and dropped it before I had
time to squeeze gratefully back. It was the first friendly contact of the night, and evidently could only be proffered in the
dark.

The chanting began for our group. The sparks were above,
around, up and down while something took place beneath
them. Soon it would be my turn to discover what that something was. Here I am, I thought, in an Indian ceremony, the
only one of my kind of skin, about to be doctored, trustfully in
the hands of Whom? Of What? And why? The why I thought I
could answer. It was my own desire, conscious or sub-
conscious to be there. I had been told about it by my friend of
the Sweat Lodge, I had dared to venture and not been turned
away. Now there was no way out, even if I wanted one. I
didn't. I was exhilarated, grateful to be where I was, "up-
standing", open to whatever came.

Something brushed my head, dropped to my shoulders,
steadied me, then I was pounded by something hard, rough,
full of heat, striking at every vital nerve-end center, every
weak or hurting place, with a tough concern that would have
its way. One of the big gourds—they seemed enormous—
brushed across my right eyelid, very gently, with a feathery
caress. I gasped. For several years I had been annoyed by a
growth on this eyelid, that hung down among my eyelashes
and when it was long enough, bothered my sight. It had been
removed many times, burned off, cut off, treated with acids, it
always came back. I couldn't put my hand up to discover what
had happened to it this time, because my shoulders were
clasped by what felt like small fingers or large claws and I
was firmly turned about for the thumping to start on my back.
It travelled from the nape of my neck down each leg in turn,
then up again to thump my kidneys twice. Each thump
seemed to bruise and penetrate the tissues with force and
heat. Each blow struck at crucial parts and their connecting
links and filled them with a painful soreness that yet was
healing.

Then whatever it was passed on to the woman next to me. She was praying aloud, and so had the man on my other side when his turn came. I realized I should have called out too, and told what needed healing, certainly I should have thanked the gourds, and whatever wore the hands or the claws. What was the matter that I could not speak when the turn was mine and I should do my part? Yet perhaps it was good to have been tongue-tied. I had not told the Medicine Man, I had not told anyone, I had not even been thinking of the ridiculous growth. . . .

"You may sit down," the voice said. This time it was the man beside me who grasped my hand, helped me to the cushion, and set me in the place where I should be. He too gave it a kindly squeeze before he dropped it, and to him too I sent a vibration of thanks. Now I was free to put a tentative finger to my eyelid and explore it carefully. The growth had disappeared. There was a small tingling place where it had certainly been. I stroked it again to make sure.

This discovery startled me more than the skillful thumping of the rest of my body, which could have been routine procedure, by men trained to work in the dark, moving on stockinged feet, (men with children's hands, or wearing claws?) using gourds charged with electricity, (but how? Cords would have been impossible. Batteries perhaps?) relying on the knowledge that the human body ails in certain areas, that any application of electric massage to those areas must be beneficial . . . but the growth on my right eyelid could hardly be seen in the magnifying light of an operating room, and at this time it had not reached the removable stage. And why had the gourd, if this was part of the routine, not swept across the other eyelid too?

What was the gourd, if it was a gourd? Even if it was worn or held by human hands, (assistants to Power Man? Tsaviaya? Power Man himself?) how could anyone, however well-trained, however able, perhaps with the help of drugs, to see in the dark, treat more than a hundred people with such rapidity, such accuracy, such penetration, and such thoroughness—in my case down to the tiny detail of an almost invisible growth among the eyelashes of one eyelid?

"You may sit down now," said the voice, and the next group in the line sat down. There were two more, then the voice said "the front line will change places with the back line." A scramble began, a groping of hands and shuffling of feet, soft exclamations and muted laughter. Eventually I found myself on the cushion again, with my two new friends on either side, glad to have the comfortable wall to lean against.

The individual part of my doctoring was over, but not my co-operation in the ceremony. Later I would relive and assimilate my experience; now it was the time to add whatever force I had received, whatever sustaining strength I could muster, to swell the power of the chant, with deliberate, concentrated, one-pointed intent, to help those being doctored, and gratefully, Those who were doctoring them.

It was difficult not to drift into a mindless state, a trance of ecstasy beneath these waves of sound, crashing, pulsating, soaring, breaking round us. Earthly time and space had gone. I was alone in vastnesses of forests, mountains, plains, the sea, yet none of these. Ancestral memories of deeper meanings behind the syllables I sang came and went before I had time to grapple them. New ones crested and fell back. Surges of Cosmic Wisdom, dimly apprehended, overwhelmed me and receded. In the center of a great whirling wheel of black flame with quickening radii erupting from it, pigmy-I held to its intent, struggling to receive, sustain, transmit currents of the Ineffable.

Naturally I failed and fell from there.

Suddenly the lights went on. I was back in a room, of all places, on the earth, of all planets, among people, of all inadequacies. Power Man was lying where we had seen him last, still bound in his blanket. He began to speak in muffled tones, so low I could not hear him clearly, but others did. There were hi-ehs and murmurs of assent. Now and then his wife repeated what was said, when it applied to all of us, as for instance that those doctored must come again the next night and for two nights more. Then Tsaviaya untied him and he sat up slowly, looking dazed. His helpers came forward and began to dismantle the oblong and remove the sacred objects. Someone brought him his shoes, and he went to sit beside his wife.

Subdued talking broke out, but no one rose. The sermony was over. Eating together was part of it, as at the Sweat Lodge. More men began to pass out paper plates and cups with plastic forks and spoons. These were put on the ground in front of us. Others took down the blankets from the doors and windows. The Power Man, his wife and Tsaviaya went outside.

"If you want to move you have to ask the Janitor", the man beside me murmured. He got up and went to the helper who was directing the distribution of the plates. This was the Janitor, evidently an important official. A few more men and boys obtained permission to go out. The rest of us stayed where we were, shifting our positions to help the circulation. The babies and some of the children were asleep. I was still grateful to have the comfort of the wall and sorry for those who had lost it. Here and there people began to stand up, keeping to their allotted space, careful not to tread on the plates in front of them.

I looked again at my friend of the Sweat Lodge, wanting to thank her for my being there. I caught her eye for a moment, but then she turned her head away. "Ah, poor us," I thought, "guilt by association." I decided not to embarrass her, to make no further overtures.

"Shall we stand?" I asked the woman beside me. "I'll help you up if you'll help me."

She didn't answer. She was now withdrawn, almost hostile. It was hard to imagine that warm handclasp in the dark. I decided not to risk standing without her help. My right leg was asleep. I stretched it into the empty place beside me and rubbed it alive.

Those who had gone outside were straggling back. The Power Man and his wife came in, and the food was served, hot when it was ladled to our dishes on the floor, cold when we would eat it, for we had to wait until everyone was served, and then for the long grace—in Arapaho—I supposed, since Power Man was saying it. When he finished we all said "oh-oh" or Amen, and started to eat. A buzz of talk began. Children escaped from their parents and ran about the room. I saw Tsaviaya scoop up a crying toddler and hold him on his lap, feeding him tidbits from his own plate. I watched those enormous hands, so deft, so tender, and wondered did they hold the gourd? But I was too tired to think, and too let down by the enormity of the transition from sacred to profane, which had startled me before in the Sweat Lodge. All I wanted now was the Sermony to end and set me free to escape into the night, outside, I thought, with a tinge of bitterness, where I belong.

It did end at last. People began to go, drifting away with nods and goodbyes. I went too. There was a long drive ahead of me, fifty-eight miles of high road, and another ten of winding dirt road, to my mountain hut. For a moment I was tempted to curl up in the car and go to sleep there where it was, on Tsaviaya's field, but I thought that might be presumptuous. Later I learned that many people did precisely that on Sermony nights. I also learned that my friend of the Sweat Lodge and those who recognized me were pleased to see me there and proud that I had come. It took me awhile to believe it.

8

The long drive went smoothly by, almost unnoticed. Stretches of the road seemed to be telescoped behind me before I reached them, one village got left out altogether. It was not my first experience of Something taking over control of my hands and feet and driving the car for me. I was always startled when this happened, and nervously grateful but it was a force I did not summon and could not consciously control.

Predawn light was on the mountains when I reached my hut. Normally I got up early to see it, especially in winter, when the snow on the crests glowed lavender-rose, but today I had only one coherent thought, sleep, recuperate, recover. I stumbled to the bed and flung my body down shoes and all.

When I woke the sun was at high noon. I was sore in every place the doctoring gourd had thumped, and other places ached in empathy, but it was a reassuring, healing sort of hurt. Underneath it my human envelope felt well, if tired. I was more interested in what had happened to its wearer.

I had studied the teachings of many spiritual leaders, lamas, gurus, and I belonged to an order devoted to the concept "Know Thyself." It seemed to me that in the strange night passed there had been a linking up of planes, a meeting of minds. Sri Aurobindo defines the mental planes as *the ordinary mind, the higher mind, the illumined mind, the transmitting mind, the intuitive mind* and *the overmind*.

My ordinary mind had been preoccupied with surface details and small discomforts, also disconcerted to discover my brash assurance where there had been habitual diffidence, an almost pathological shyness, mostly in flight towards safe solitude. My higher mind, absorbed in the unfolding of the ceremony, was sorting out impressions, making comparisions, trying to grasp and retain knowledge above the limitations of conscious, logical thought. My illumined mind was in a state of spiritual ease and happiness, of enthusiasm (as the Greeks understood the word), a sudden awakening to Truth, without compulsion to dissect or even understand it; coherence might come later, through the transmitting mind, vibrating in what Sri Aurobindo calls "a luminous sweep". My intuitive mind whirled in fragmented illumination, lightnings flashed from silence, spiritual fireworks, evaporating, reforming, points of recognition gone as soon as come, too rapid for collected thought or memory. My overmind was above analysis, but there had been a time in the fathomless dark and the vortex of sound when Pigmy-I soared to the edge of that "plane of cosmic consciousness without the loss of the individual."

I was still reflecting and sorting out these myriad impressions as I stripped and went to the round horse trough I called my guru bath. It was fed by water from a mountain stream, pure and icy cold. Here I did my ablutions, three times a day, dawn, noon and sunset, praying, face to the mountain. I had missed dawn, but it was now high twelve, or thereabouts, by the sun.

"Great Spirit, Friend of the Soul . . . ."

"Open your eyes in me, that I may see, open your ears in me that I may hear, open your compassion in me that I may have compassion upon all that you have made. And give me understanding of the ceremony."

All those mental planes, those Minds, sat in council within my earthly brain, in the small room of the skull. Already they were drawing apart, dissolving the rainbow bridges, widening tenuous space. It was no use clinging to them, or trying to retain their revelations, any more than trying to remember the words or the music of the chants I had known so perfectly . . .these belonged to their own places, and could only be apprehended there. I must accept this desolate sense of loss and limitation to the three-dimensional plane, until time or circumstances should restore me to the Truth.

"His absence be the child I carry
All days and all years."

I must turn to images, to inadequate words, to contain the uncontainable, concealed in the upper Fire.

"Eternally and this night he will deliver me."

I must be content with that assurance and those substituted secrets, until the next ascension toward Reality.

Meanwhile "this night", the second night of the Ceremony was ahead, and there were preparations to be made. I must cook a dish of food, find a more comfortable cushion, and go to a far-off town to buy the things I had been told to bring.

9

When I arrived at the yardgoods counter of J.C. Penny's there were several Indians there, whose faces I recognized, all buying the same quantities of different colored materials. I joined them in time to hear the clerk say, "I'm sorry, we're out of green, but here is a pretty stripe. . ."

"Must be green."

"I'm sorry."

Then a man asked for the same amount of red, and the clerk measuring it out asked curiously: "What are you going to do with all this stuff? Is there a Pow-wow?"

Heads were shaken.

"No Pow-wow."

One woman who seemed to be a respected Elder, from the way the others deferred to her, said: "My cousin makes quilts.'

The mystified clerk stopped questioning, and everyone relaxed.

It was a true statement, no doubt, since one must tell the truth, especially before a doctoring ceremony, but a cousin

making quilts and the purpose for this material were unre-
lated subjects. I could not help smiling. She looked at me and
smiled back. I had a sudden warm feeling of acceptance, but
one mustn't count too much on its lasting. It was my turn to
tease the clerk by buying the Indians' improbable material,
with my white face. She looked at me suspiciously, but fortunately she didn't ask me anything, so I didn't have to find an
ingenious phrase about the shirt of my uncle or the parasol of
my aunt.

The Indians left together and I followed them to the reservation. Here everything was as it had been the night before, cars
in the parking lot and a long line outside the tipi. Did one
present the Pipe a second time? No, it was merely to deliver
the things we had been told to get. We gave them to Power
Man's wife, and went across the field with our cushions and
food, to the Ceremony House.

Here we took the places we had sat in before, but this time I
knew that later I would rest my back against the comfortable
wall, and this time my cushion was plumper, and this time the
woman beside me smiled and said "Hello", as I sat down, and
the man beside me nodded. I saw my friend of the Sweat
Lodge. This time she looked back at me and lifted her hand in
a surreptitious greeting.

"They were wondering whether I'd come back," I thought,
"and they seem to be glad I came."

We sat in silence while the preparations began. There were
some differences, not in the preparation but in the atmosphere. There was a blue-grey dusky light in the corners of the
room, which persisted behind my eyelids, even when the
lights were on and the doors and windows blanketed.
People's faces were less stern, less strained. Their bodies
might be as tired and as sore as mine, but our minds and
hearts were reassured. We rested in our assigned, familiar
places, as one settles into the theatre seat, the plane seat, the
now-corner of anywhere, ours "for the duration", where it has
been decided it is right for us to be.

Even the way in which we drank the purifying water,
smudged ourselves with the sacred smoke and took the sprigs
of sage had a difference about it, the ease of familiarity,
almost of pleasure. Otherwise all proceeded as before, the

laying out of the guardian wall, the placing of the sacred
objects at the four corners with the colored cloths, the binding
of the Power Man into his turquoise blanket with the thunderbird design, his descent to the floor, the protective blessing
Tsaviaya gave him with the burning sweet grass, and the
sudden total darkness, anticipated but still startling.

Then the great outburst of drumming and the chants began
and they different too, not in rhythm or in volume but in
essence. It seemed to me, as I listened to the strange, nasal,
high-pitched sounds coming from my vocal chords, that this
time we were evoking a different kind of spirit, not necessarily
from a higher plane than Those who had come before, but
from a different Ray.

When it was my turn to be doctored I knew that this was so.
The hands that turned me about were talons, with no suggestion of fingers, and the gourds which had thumped me were
great feathers, enormous wings, travelling the length of my
body, unerringly beating the sick places, reinforcing, renew-
ing the whole. Hot air fanned out from them, curling round my
head. This time I remembered to shout my gratitude aloud,
under cover of the chanting.

When the doctoring was over, the drumming and the singing died away, not abruptly like the first time, instead it was
dwindling in a final humming sound, a murmured
Ommmmm. A whirring cut the silence, a gust of air swept over
me, something large descended to the right. There was a
muffled cry from the man beside me, then silence, through
which I heard the steady pulsating beat of enormous wings,
circling high above us in the night sky, displacing the air in
rhythmic sweeps, round. . . .round. . . . round. . . . Grandfather Eagle inspecting the people, giving them his blessing
before he flew away?

The lights went on, the sky was gone, we were in the
ceilinged room again. Power Man, freed of his blanket, was
kneeling in the center of the oblong. The blanket was covering
the head and shoulders of the man next to me. It was that
which I had heard whirring down. He emerged from beneath it
and began to fold it, slowly, methodically, Thunderbird upward. Thunderbird! Most surely what we heard circling above

us must have been the Thunderbird, the Messenger, the Mediator, the Great Being representing the Four Powers of the Creator, the Four Old Men in charge of the Universe, the Bird of God. It was his representative, Grandfather Eagle, who had visited the Sweat Lodge.

Again we were sitting in our places, waiting for the food to be served, the grace to be said. Again we ate, and after a decent interval took up our cushions, said goodbye and left. My neighbor, honored by the blanket covering him, walked beside me toward the cars. His step was proud, he radiated joy. Half way across the field he stopped.

"You come tomorrow? Two more time." He hesitated, then he said shyly, looking down, "that way you get blessing, too."

"I know," I said. "I am very blessed."

"Share," he said, "share everything."

We said goodnight and turned away. My car was at the further end of the field. When I reached it I was sharply tempted to curl up on the back seat and go to sleep, but I thought of the cleansing bath, the plants expecting care, the need to stretch in my accustomed place, properly oriented, head to north, with the hope that during sleep the day's experiences might be sorted out for me.

As I started the long drive fatigue left, and again I felt my hands taken over by the Supernatural Steerer. Lines and images of wings began to come to me.

"Risen with healing in His wings."

"My soul, there is a country
Far beyond the stars,
Where stands a winged sentry. . . ."

I had spent many years studying comparative religions, deeply enough to have layers of related symbols in the storeroom of the mind, to be able to co-relate them and to quote them. I knew that in ancient Syria the eagle with human arms stood for sun-worship; that he conducted souls to immortality and in general went between the earth and unseen worlds. I knew that the Christians regarded the eagle as a messenger from heaven, that Theodoret compared him to the spirit of prophecy, and Saint Jerome said he was the symbol of Ascension and of prayer. . . . the eagle's flight because of its height

and swiftness . . . prayer rising to the Great Spirit, answering
Grace descending to the world. In Christian churches he is
found bearing the weight of great bronze lecterns with the
open Bible upon them, signifying that the eagle carries the
Logos, the Word of Life to earth. I knew that the Bible is full of
him.

"They that wait upon the Lord shall renew their strength;
they shall mount up with wings as eagles."

"The bird of the air shall carry the voice and that which hath
wings shall tell the matter."

I knew that in ancient Persia he was Siena, "the ever
blessed, glorious and mighty bird whose wings dim the very
heavens."

I knew all this theoretically, but I had never before come
into actual contact with him from the three dimensional
plane, nor realized what it meant for him to be the messenger,
one of the messengers, between planes and worlds. Now I
would study the Thunderbird, "the winged creature which
crowns the totem pole and represents the Great Creator or the
four Great Creative Forces."

Four was significant. The four elements, earth, water, air
and fire, each with its own angel, shown with wings like a
bird; the four Archangels, Gabriel, Michael, Raphael, Azrael,
the messenger, the warrior, the healer, the lord of death; the
four apostles, Matthew, Mark, Luke and John, Saint John de-
picted as an eagle; I must study *four*, symbol of earth, of
terrestrial space, the square, the four directions, the four seasons, the four stages of human life; materialized energy . . .
all of these under the outspread wings of the Thunderbird.

The car brought me to a stop outside my door, much sooner
than I could have reached it normally, without the Steerer's
help. I stumbled out and stood beneath the stars. The Milky
Way was directly above, and as I stretched my arms upward
in gratitude that I lived where I could see a vast expanse of
sky, I thought I saw something flying between me and the
stars.

I knew the Song of the Stars, an old Algonquin poem, *Nilun
pesazmuk elintaquik*:

We are the stars which sing,

We sing with our light.
We are the birds of fire,
We fly across the heaven,
Our light is a star,
We make a road for Spirits,
A road for the Great Spirit.

On that road the Thunderbird is travelling, and how many others. It would not have surprised me to see Jacob's Ladder, or Dante's great stairway of created being, rising heaven-ward, or Ruysbroeck's *Seven Steps of the Ladder of Spiritual Love*, or some other vision. . . . but my cup was full, and it could not have contained another drop.

10

The third night of the Sermonies surprised me from the start. Everyone seemed in a state of happy this-plane bustle. Children were laughing and playing round the door of the Sermony House, beneath benevolent glances from the elders. There seemed to be a sort of Christmas Eve atmosphere of goodwill and conspiracy, unlike the solemn awe of the preceding nights.

A little boy ran up to me, grinning and hopping with excitement.

"Grandfather Clown come in," he said, "much candy."

A woman nodded and smiled at me. "Grandfather Clown do all things funny, upside down, make people laugh."

I smiled back, to show I understood, in part at least, the function of the Clowns. This must be Happiness Clown, if he made people laugh. The other Clown Amerindians have is Sadness Clown. They serve the same purpose, to lighten the burden of sorrow. Happiness Clown takes away sadness by making people laugh. "He'll dance like crazy till his bloomers fall down." He is the fun-maker, like the Koshare or Kurena, or the Chiffonete, privileged to do or say anything, especially to make fun of authority. The Chiffonete "whoop and yell, always with the restrained musical call of the Indian; they run up and down ladders and in and out of houses, bringing laughter wherever they go. All day they run around, making 'wise-cracks'. But they have also great powers of healing and are the performers of the fertility rites.

Sadness Clown is more sacred than Happiness Clown and has more power than Medicine Man. Sadness Clown "tries to take away your sadness. If you're sitting there sad or lonely he'll come and sit by you. As he looks at you, you can see him pull the sadness out of you and take it on himself." In this way he is the eternal scapegoat, the sacrifice.

As I waited in my place on the floor of the Sermony House, I tried to recall what I remembered of clowns and their corrective, cathartic function in all civilizations. They had their origin, or one of their strong tributaries, in Greek comedy, descended from Dionysian rites in which wild choruses like the Koshare dancers, mimed the fertility of the earth with phallic symbols. Then there were the medieval clowns and Kings' jesters, like Henry the First's Rahere, whose ghost walked the chapel built for him in London. Later came Shakespeare's immortal fools, in which he merges the two kinds, Happiness and Sadness in one. The French still keep them separate, Pierrot-qui-rit, Pierrot qui pleure.

Then comes the further stage, the Clown that becomes the Fool, the Parsifal.

But there was no more time for analogies, for ponderings. The preparations were complete, the room sealed off, the magnetized oblong laid, Power Man and his assistants in place, the people silent and alert, the children quieted, the darkness, the drums, the chanting of the Come-In Song, begun.

Through this and the healing songs to follow there were subtle differences of rhythm hard to define, except perhaps a jocular down-to-earth vibration fleeting here and there. The healing was done with gourds as on the first night, but here again there was a difference, the blows were hard and playful, and followed a different sequence. When I expected my knees to be pounded, it was the elbows, and when I expected to be turned, there were blows on the top of my head and on each cheek.

After the healing, when we were all in our changed places, Power Man spoke from his place on the ground.

"He wants to dance. He says four more."

The drumming and the songs broke out again in a new rhythm and again 'jocular' was the word I found for it. A woman laughed and cried out as apparently Clown seized her. There were stamping sounds, and stumbling and whirling in different parts of the room. I heard a woman say "I can't, I'm too old," to no avail. He danced with her longer than with the others, to accompanying gasps and laughter. The singing and the drumming went on imperturbably, over all the cries and laughter, the thumping, and then as he danced alone, bounding, stamping, striking the ground with something sharp, little cries went up. He was hitting out with whatever he held, as the Koshare do with their yucca sticks, fools with their baubles. I felt a sharp tap on my shoulder and cried out, too, for I knew that response was part of the ritual.

Suddenly the four songs ended. In the silence that followed a new sound began, the sharp crackle of hard candies hitting the floor, the walls, the ceiling. Children shrieked and scrambled to pick them up, without actually leaving their places. The woman beside me said "Get some," and I reached forward to pick up those in front of me. Then the children, and some of the adults began to shout: "We don't want your candy. We don't like you. We don't thank you for being here. We don't need you. We want you to go away" and so on. To Grandfather Clown you must say the opposite of what you mean, as he says and does the opposite of what he means. This is also true of the Little Men of the Mountains, who seem to be Grandfather Clowns in miniature. I was later told they hugely enjoy this form of address and do their work of healing with more joy and energy, the more they are insulted.

The fun lasted for awhile, then the drums rolled softly, silence returned. Power Man said something in Arapaho. His wife repeated it in English.

"He says you're a poor lot of no-goods here. The children are all asleep. Nobody to dance with. He says he'll stay now. He don't bless you, he don't wish you well. He won't see you again."

"We don't want you to stay. We don't thank you, Grandfather. We don't want to see you again," we all shouted.

There was a tremendous thump at the door, and he was gone. The lights went up. Power Man was in his blanket on the floor. After the dismantling of the sacred oblong he was untied and given his shoes. He went to sit in his place beside his wife. The children compared their handfuls of candy with one another and began to eat them.

"Eat," said the woman beside me, so I did. I was glad I had only found a few, for they were the white man's poisonous cheap candy, with red coloring, artificial additives and, of course, white sugar. Still, so strongly blessed and in such a place they must be purified and freed from harm. They would have been smudged with sage before they were used and sage is a strong antidote.

It was a pity nothing better could be found. What, I wondered, did Grandfather Clown toss to his children in the old days, and why could it not be used today? The wrong things in the white culture have overwhelmed the red, with none, or too little, of the best the white civilizations have to offer. It is pitiful to see in the Indian museums, among the beautiful treasures of the Red Man, the apalling, degrading junk representing the Whites, when there could be at least prints of the glory that was Greece, the grandeur that was Rome and all the superb works of art since. Beethoven might be played instead of rock. A combination of the good in each tradition would be a better environment for the growth of new generations.

Grace followed, given this time, not by Power Man or Tsaviaya, but by one of the men who sat with them, in front of a big drum. We ate, and there was more conversation, some joking and laughter, before we drifted out with soft goodbyes.

11

On the fourth night of the Sermonies, awe and silence returned to the preliminaries. People smiled but did not speak unless they had to, and then in a whisper. The children were on their best behavior, still and silent. There were physical reasons for this. Our bodies were stiff, sore and very tired, but mostly we were subdued by something in the atmosphere, vibrations of expectancy.

The woman beside me murmured "Head Man coming in tonight!" I wondered Who or What this might be. It was explained when Power Man's wife leaned forward to interpret what he said, after he was lowered to the ground, before the lights went out.

"Grandfather Buffalo saying he will come in tonight to check on us."

There were gratified murmurs and rustlings as we adjusted ourselves and the singing began. The Come-in song was

different, heavier, with a more solemn substance, less entre-
aty than on the first night, but the healing songs were those
we had sung the first time, and the pounding was done with
the big gourds. Deep into the sore parts of my body the penetration went, hurting and assuaging the cells and atoms prepared to receive it. Also this time there were extra thumps on
the centers of the chakras.

When it was over and all had been doctored, there came a
greater, more aware silence than even those of the preceding
nights. It lasted to the limits of our endurance. It was broken
by a tremendous blow on the door, a sound as though the door
itself had fallen into splinters and was being crushed beneath
an enormous force, impossible to oppose. This was followed
by unexpected delicate clicking sounds of rhythmic footsteps.
I opened my eyes to see small circles of golden light moving
forward on the floor toward the oblong. Here they paused, and
then, although I could no longer see them, obstructed by the
line in front, I knew that they were proceding the length of the
border; I saw them again going along the short side, and
along the side where Power Man's wife, the drummers and the
singers sat, and back by the far short side to where they
began. Now there was a pawing sound and another small
crash, and they were in the center where Power Man lay. He
began to speak in a low, strong voice, interpreted by his wife.
"He say he pleased. All going well here."

"Hy-eh, Oh-ho, Hmmm," the people said.

"He say the doctored ones o-k now."

"Hy-eh, hy-eh!"

"He say rest four days. Go easy on yourselves. He say some
people here need to stop what they were doing wrong and
start again."

"Hy-eh! Hy-eh! Thank you, Grandfather."

"He say the woman with the child sick in the hospital need
to make green pouches. That little boy been very sick. Be
better now."

"Hy-eh! Hy-eh! Hy-eh!"

"He say he'll send an old man to be with him now."

"Thank you, Thank you, Grandfather."

"He say most all good people here, but some don't do so
good."

Power Man grunted and said something rapidly. His wife hesitated, then repeated in Arapaho, not English, what was said. Someone cried out, someone sobbed.

"He say he bless you now, then he must go."

"Hy-eh! Hy-eh! Thank you, thank you, Grandfather."

Something ponderous passed by us. I opened my hands and bowed my head to receive the blessing, and indeed I felt it, and knew when it had dealt with me and the woman beside me. When the tour was completed and all the people blessed, there was a short silence, then another blow at the door, a single sharp rap, a final clicking stamp. Grandfather Buffalo left us. A wave of sighing breath went round the room, carrying love, carrying farewell.

After another silence the lights went on. No one moved as we absorbed the shock of the shattering descent from plane to plane, and made the bereft adjustment. After awhile Power Man's assistants went to release him from the blanket with the Great Thunderbird on it.

One of them tied his shoes and another helped him up. He seemed spent and weakened as he went to sit by his wife, who smiled and murmured to him and passed him something which he put into his mouth. The deft dismantling went on, for the last time. The doors were opened for the night air to rush in. The food was served, the long grace said and presently we ate. During all this time no one spoke.

Presently the children broke the spell, the small ones running about and the older ones whispering and giggling. Power Man stood up, unobtrusively making for the door. He disappeared. His wife and attendants followed. Sermonies were over for this time.

Still the people sat, loath to leave, but after awhile we went, in little groups, spent and satisfied, to our waiting cars, and, if we might have them, our four days of rest. Many of us had far to go and must set out at once, sure of protection on the way and that all would be well with us.

So now, I thought, as I drove through the dawn, toward my mountain hut, I have all these things to study, to ponder, to weave into my being. And once more I gave thanks.

12

During the rest of the year I went regularly to Tsaviaya's Sweat Lodge and to the Sermonies whenever Power Man came from his reservation to conduct them. I seemed to be an accepted part of the Red community. Some of the Sweat people came to see me, many nodded and smiled on the streets or in the stores. Once I was walking with a local doctor's wife when a passing group waved and said "hi's" to me from across the street. One detached herself and came to tell me under cover of laughter and friendly banalities, a quick murmured 'Doctoring Sweat tonight.' She nodded politely to my white friend, said 'see you, be good now' to me and crossed back to the others.

We walked on for a moment in silence, then the doctor's wife said wistfully, "I've been trying for thirty years to know the Indians, and I don't get anywhere. What was all that about?"

"Oh, I said, "I helped her with a couple of forms to be filled in. That's Annie Perow."

"I know. She's a patient of ours, and her daughter works in John's office. I used to take people to her house when she was still making baskets. I see her round all the time. We say hello, and that's it. And it's the same with all the others. I thought it was because no white could be accepted as a friend, but now. . . ."

Now there was me, the rest of the thought went, a new-comer, a Janey-come-lately, or at least more lately than she. I remembered when her husband had said to me quite seri-ously "You must *never* go onto the reservation after dark, it isn't safe," and she had added "and not in daylight, unless you go with someone, or tell someone you're going."

It happened to be a day when there was a Sweat Lodge. What, I wondered, would they have thought if they could have seen me, sitting cross-legged on the tule, worshipping with the Indians they had 'always wanted to know', a stone's throw from their impressive house?

"I've been very lucky," I said. "I do their papers for them, and I live in a little hut a lot like theirs. They're probably in awe of you." But I could see she was still hurt and puzzled.

This doctoring Sweat was the first I went to, and I wasn't sure what to expect. I prepared as I did for other sweats, and took a casserole of rice and tomatoes from the garden patch. When I arrived I found this wasn't necessary. For Doctoring Sweats the patient's family provides all the food, but others had brought extras too and my offering was graciously ac-cepted.

The man to be doctored was a construction worker who had fallen from a scaffolding and hurt his back. He was carried into the Sweat Lodge and put down on the tule reeds, with his head next to Tsaviaya. Then we all filed in, his wife next to him, then his family beside her, men and women together on the women's side. Tsaviaya's face and hands were streaked with red, from the powdered stone used for medicine "paint". His long eagle feathers were lying on a bed of sage beside him and there were other objects there. The sick man's 'flags' were fastened to the ceiling toward the west.

When the rocks were in place, Tsaviaya said to the man "Don't be afraid to holler. Cry out loud. Tell the Grandfather all what you need." And to his wife, "When I say 'turn him' you help to put him on his stomach, and when I say 'cover him' you spread the blanket out."

To us he said, "I ask you people kindly to pray for this man."

"Oh-ho, Oh-ho," in the usual guttural chorus.

"You can pray for your family, your relations and your friends. But that's all."

"Oh-ho, Oh-ho."

"If it gets too hot go way down. It's going to be hot."

"Oh-ho, Oh-ho."

"Everybody ready?"

"Oh-ho."

The door flaps went down and we were in darkness. A storm of prayer broke out and the Come-in Song began, urgent and imploring. There were more rocks than usual, all of them red hot. The pyramid towered above the sunken pit. The heat was searing, almost beyond bearing. We knew it would get worse, especially in the third round. We also knew it must be so if the man were to be helped, that whatever Spirits came in to do the healing required this. "Grandfathers want it *hot*." So while we buried our faces in the handfuls of sage, and bowed our heads to the ground, and drew in scorching breath, we sang sturdily, fervently, breaking off only to pray and now and then to shout, sometimes to scream, but not to relieve a physical agony, this was, if there could be such a thing, a *religious* scream. "I cried unto the Lord with all my soul, and (of course) He heard me." So it would be here, for this man and his family and, an afterthought, for us.

When the round was over, we were all in little crouching heaps, and so we stayed, until the steam had rushed out both the doors. The sick man was covered in his blanket, one hand clutching sage to his face. His wife—she was the only one upright—patted his feet. Tsaviaya lay sideways, his face to the opening, his eyes closed. He was a very heavy man, and as he told us sometimes when we came out of a sweat saying "Hot!" to each other, "Sweat *always* hot and hard on me!"

But some Sweats were gentle, for us if not for him. When a newcomer came, or a baby for its first round—the equivalent of a christening—there were differences in the heat. It has been very hot for me, and barely warm for my neighbors, or I have been in the comfortable 'gentle glow' once prescribed for 'ladies', and my neighbors have been gasping and barely able to make it. It depends, I suppose, on what has taken place between the sweats, and whether or not you are still in a state of grace. But a Doctoring Sweat is always hard and hot for everybody. It is a privilege to take part in one, but also a sacrifice, which brings its own blessing. The family and friends of the patient have the comfort of being able to contribute something tangible, an outpouring of sweat, to the prayers and the healing. So often the ordeal of those who have to watch the people whom they love suffer, is deepened by the helpless feeling that there is nothing they can do to help. In the Doctoring Sweat there is.

Before the second round began, Tsaviaya sent the dipperful of water round the circle.

"Drink all you want," he said. "After this no water."

We drank and poured it on ourselves. Tsaviaya sprinkled it over the patient and poured a dipperful on his own head. Then the flaps were shut, the prayers and the song begun.

Now we could hear the strokes of Tsaviaya's great Eagle Feather beating the sick man's back. At every downward rhythmic stroke the heat in the Sweat Lodge increased, so that it seemed as though we too were being flayed. The Singers carried the singing steadily without a gasp or falter. The rest of us sang between the strokes. The sick man cried to the Grandfathers for help. Now and then he screamed and the song rose louder. Tsaviaya was 'talking' in high pitched tones. On and on it went, until when no hope of conclusion remained to us, it stopped.

"Bless yourselves."

We did, to the sick man's sobbing.

"Hy-eh!"

The flaps went up, the steam rushed out, we kept our heads down as we tried to breathe. The sick man lay shuddering and moaning beneath the blanket which his valiant wife draped over him. All through the doctoring this woman remained upright, cross-legged on the tule, suffering with her husband. She was nearest to the heat of the downbeating wings yet she sat straight and still, head and face uncovered, ready to attend to Tsaviaya's instructions. He was lying with his face outside the flap, gulping the cool air.

No one asked to leave. I knew instinctively that from a Doctoring Sweat no one could leave, as no one could ask for water. I knew too that the third round ahead of us would be the hardest. After that the give-thanks round, the Pipe, and then. . . . but it was best to concentrate on *now* and pray that one might endure and be of help. There was past experience to draw on. Never, no matter what the heat, had I been burned or blistered or harmed in any way. On the contrary, each Sweat had brought me nearer to good health. The balance in my body, lost by illness and anxiety, was being gradually regained. So this discomfort could not permanently hurt me and it too would pass. But that was not the right way to think about it. I should be praying harder for the sick man. It would have been easier if I had known him as a friend or even an acquaintance; yet I did know him, after these two rounds, as I knew everyone in the Sweat. We shared an other-plane unspoken companionship.

"Everybody ready?"

"Oh-ho. Oh-ho."

Were we? We had to be. I shifted a little to expose the least scalded parts to the steam. The flaps went down and the third round began. The chanting and the beating, the sobbing and the screaming began again, but now there was a new sound, of heavy stamping feet passing round the fire in a slow deliberate dance. Tsaviaya, I thought, in a Medicine Dance, but then who was doctoring the patient? For the fanning of the feathers went on, and Tsaviaya's guttural voice was coming from his corner. Someone else must be dancing, but there had been no movement in the circle for "someone else" to stand up.

My eyes were closed, my face was buried in the handful of sage, I held my breath as the heavy steps drew near and whoever it was went by. Singing faltered as the footsteps passed, and began again when they were by. Now the last water splashed onto the rocks, the last steam seared us, the last cries went up, the last pattings for the "bless-you", and as we grovelled, spent, the flaps went up.

The sick man sobbed beneath his blanket, he retched and began to vomit.

"Good! Good!" voices cried. "Get rid of it! Don't be ashamed." Tsaviaya said something from his corner, lying with his face to the air. The man's wife patted his feet and rearranged the blanket. Then we all lay still until Tsaviaya sat up, the signal for us to struggle somehow into position for the fourth round. This was the farewell and the thanking-you-for-blessing song. It rose, slow and stately, as the more gentle steam flowed over us. There was solemnity and awe and sadness in it. The sick man lay quietly, not sobbing anymore, not vomiting. The doctoring part of the Sweat was over. We were being blessed and prepared for the coming in of the Pipe.

The round was over. It seemed comparatively short, but we were glad to rest and pant the good air in. Then Tsaviaya said "Clear up in front of you," and we sat up, scraping the ground clear of sage and ash, straightening ourselves, tidying the towels. The sick man lay on his back, his wife smoothing the blanket, and clearing the ground in front of him.

The Pipe came in and began its round. It seemed a different tobacco, stronger than usual, as the smoke swirled about the circle, going always towards the patient. Tsaviaya finished smoking, collected his things and went out. The rest of us crept after him leaving the man and his family in the lodge. Presently they carried him out in his blanket, and took him to Tsaviaya's house.

He did not come to eat with us, nor did his wife, but the others did, and his son said the grace. Then Tsaviaya said "Grandfathers want three more doctoring sweats, tomorrow, next day, next." It was understood that we would all come.

We did. On the third night the man sat up to smoke the Pipe. On the fourth night, he walked out of the Sweat Lodge by himself, and went to Tsaviaya's house, leaning on his wife's arm. He came to eat with us and tried to sit on the hard seat by the table, but Tsaviaya made him lie down on the battered sofa for the sick and the old. His wife helped him to eat. I had grown to love and respect this woman to whom I never spoke, for her dignity, for her courage and her faith. She had a beautiful face, and when she smiled, as she did now, there was no need for words.

Tsaviaya announced a Grandfathers' Sweat, that is a thanksgiving Sweat, for blessings received, to be held the next day, in the morning, so that the visitors could be on their way. Again it was understood that we would all be there.

I have heard people say that Indians are unreliable, that they take too many days off from their work and can't be depended upon to turn up when they're expected, and that the excuses they give—when they give any—are usually absurd or obviously untrue. "They don't know what it is to *work* at anything."

There might be an explanation, but who would be willing to give it? What troubles might ensue?

13

For many months I went to the Sweat Lodges, the Sermonies, and the Doctoring Sweats to which I was summoned. I studied the books that came my way and meditated on the passages that sprang off the page to me. I was deep into *The Sacred Pipe*, Black Elk's Account of the Seven Rites of the Oglala Sioux, transcribed by Joseph Epes Brown, when it came to me that I should ask for a pipe.

At first I recoiled, abashed, and told myself severely that this was an example of impulsive enthusiasm, not to say brashness. But the suggestion persisted, until it grew into conviction. I asked the Grandfathers to guide me, and at one of the Sermonies I approached Power Man's wife.

"May a woman have a pipe?"

"Yes."

"I mean a woman like me, with only a little Indian blood?"

She smiled.

"Ask him."

So I went to Power Man, and asked him, "May I have a pipe?"

"Why do you want it?"

I summoned courage.

"When I first presented pipe to you, I could not speak, aloud."

He nodded.

"But inside I was asking to be a healer of miseries."

He said nothing, and I went on, braving the rebuke to come.

"People come to me for help, those who cannot come to you or to Tsaviaya."

He was silent.

"Whites, for whom perhaps this is not the way. Yet they need help. I do give them what I can, what I have learned in other ways, and in the Sweat, without telling, but I thought perhaps if I had a pipe . . ."

He said "Women without a husband, may have a family pipe. You are asking for a Working Pipe. That is a different thing."

I said, "I know."

He thought for a long moment while I stood head bowed before him, then he smiled at me gently.

"Present your pipe," he handed me his to fill, "and ask the Grandfathers. They will answer."

So I filled his beautiful pipe and gave it to him, saying the ritual words, and after them "I humbly ask may I have a working pipe to help the people whom you send to me."

He smoked it slowly, and the smoke came in great whirling circles round my head. When he had finished smoking, he looked up at me and said "Come again in three days time and ask me. I shall be here till Sunday."

I thanked him and went away, trembling, trying to control my shaking knees, trying to walk steadily before the others now waiting to consult him. Composure returned as I drove home. After all, I told myself, the Grandfathers take intent into account. If They tell me no, I shall have done what I could, and They will find other ways for me to help—herbs, candles, mantras.

I was using some of these already, but there was more, much more to know. They would help me to learn. I decided to go on a three-day fast (as I understood fasting then) with purification and meditation. I began in the circular bath, giving over its healing power to this purpose. I fasted from books, music, speech, except for what had to be said each day to those who came and went. I ate nothing and drank only fruit juice and mountain tea.

I said "Yes!" to the Great Spirit, "Thy Will, not mine," I said it with joy, lifting the question up, offering myself to be used, with or without the pipe, in any way, sometimes adding, "May I fulfill the mission You have sent me here, this life, to do." It was a long, strange three days, and four nights, during which the world seemed at a standstill, yet everything around me grew more beautiful, more alive, aware, but also waiting, a time of lull, of lying fallow.

On the third day I went back to Power Man. There was no one waiting outside his tipi. The doorflap was open. He was sitting on the tule reeds, facing it.

"Come in, come in."

I stooped to enter and stood before him.

"Sit down."

It was the first time that I had been asked to sit in the tipi. I took my place on the reeds, with enough distance between us so that he did not need to turn his head to look at me.

He said slowly, "Grandfathers say 'yes,' you may have your pipe."

"Hy-eh! Hy-eh! Thank you, my Grandfathers."

"It is a serious thing. Much work. Much taking care."

"Hy-eh."

"You must prepare yourself."

"I will."

"You must get the stone, also."

"It comes from Pipestone in Minnesota, doesn't it?"

"Yes. You can go there?"

"I will." I didn't see how, but I knew it would be made possible.

"When you get it, give offerings. The Pipe-maker will look for the stem and make it."

"Hy-eh."

"Then you wait."

He smiled his gentle, humorous smile. "Later we talk more." He waved toward the door. So I went out, filled with joy. I even danced a few steps and heard a chuckle behind me.

I drove home wondering "Minnesota! How to get there?" I had no money. My car was old and rickety, it would never stand the journey. I did have a credit card. Perhaps I could borrow someone's better car. But the stone would be expensive, and the offerings, and no doubt the food for a special sweat. I had nothing to sell, but the typewriter, and I had learned that we must keep our working tools. I took in typing for a living, and already had almost as much as I could handle. It brought in very little, just enough for daily needs. I had also learned that our needs are taken care of, through the abundance of the Divine resources, but not, necessarily extras and wants. Was this an extra? It was certainly a want, how deep a one!

But, when the time was right, I might have a Pipe!

That night I slept better than I had for many days. Next morning I had just finished breakfast, when a friend of mine arrived, with an asking expression. I had helped her in the past. I waited.

"Will you do me a great favor?"

"If I can."

"That's the point. Can you get away for awhile? I have to go east, and I have to take the truck because I'm bringing back a lot of things. I need someone to drive me and I can't think of anyone I can bear to go with but you!" She looked at me pleadingly. "We'd have fun on the way. I don't have to race. We could camp in some of the national forests. Oh, do say you'll come."

"How far do you have to go?"

"It's in Indiana."

"I'll go if you will do me a favor in return."

"Anything. What is it?"

"I want to go to the Pipestone National Monument in Minnesota. Could we manage that?"

"Of course. It's almost right on the way. I've always wanted to go there. Will you really come?"

Would I? Oh Grandfathers!

"I can share the driving, and help with the gas." Now it was I who was eager.

"Fine, but you don't need to share the gas, when you're going for me. I'll do all the expenses." Oh Grandfathers!

"When do you want to go?"

"As soon as we can. Would Tuesday suit you?"

It would, though there was still the problem of the money for the stone. But that would surely also be taken care of so I said, "Tuesday I'll be ready." She went away, dancing a few steps as I had from Power Man.

On Monday, when I was beginning, inspite of my faith, to be a little anxious, a check for $137.89 came in, on royalties for a book I had written some years before, which now, the letter said, would have a paperback edition in England. It was enough to take care of everything. I went up on the mountain to give thanks, and roll on Mother Earth in blissful gratitude.

Next day we set out. I found to my further pleasure that my companion preferred the back roads to large expressways, and had no sense of pressure, or of proper eating times. There was a camper top on the truck, an old mattress and two sleeping bags, a little cooking stove, and she had stocked up on provisions. We rolled away in style.

The journey was pleasant, and protected from any untoward events, or problems, as it would be under the aegis of the Grandfathers. We talked of how it must have been through the centuries for the tribes living in the west to make the journey, on foot, and to return carrying enough stone for their needs. I did not tell her why I wanted stone, but only that I had to take some to a friend.

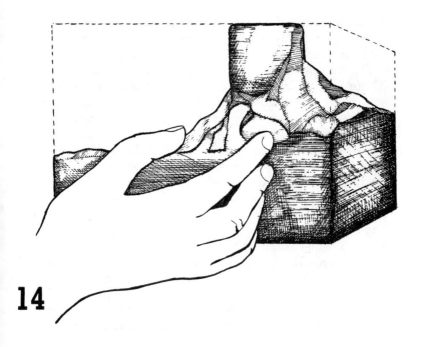

14

When I first went to Pipestone it was possible to buy small blocks of the red catlinite in the Headquarters Building of the National Monument. Later this practice was discontinued. Commercialism set in. It was more profitable to carve fake "peace"-pipes and junky little objects for the tourists, out of the sacred stone, than to give, or sell, needed blocks to a genuine Pipe-maker, to be used in the traditional way.

Permission to quarry, fashion and sell pipestone within the monument has been reserved by law to American Indians, who still work in the pits in the late summer and fall, as their ancestors did. The stone is quarried in the same pits where for centuries representatives of all the tribes journeyed to obtain the sacred clay for their pipeheads.

There was once a seashore there, where a deposit of muddy clay was buried in the sand. Pressure, heat and chemical action changed the sand into quartzite and the clay into pipestone, smooth and soapy to the touch, in contrast to the rough covering. I bought four blocks, 8x6 inches long and 2½ inches thick, from the Sioux official in charge of sales.

We did not want to walk the trail past the quarries to the 'Great Stony Face' and 'The Oracle' arranged for the tourists swarming round us. A year later I returned out of season to discover the strong, charged vibrations of the brooding spirit there, and once, having the place to myself, I smoked by the waterfall where many must have smoked before me, but this time I was content to follow the legend of the coming of the Sacred Pipe to the Sioux, presented in a film.

The version was the same as the one given in full in *The Sacred Pipe* and in the pamphlet put out by the Monument. The Pipe was brought to the Sioux by a Sacred White Buffalo Woman, who explained it to them, holding it up, stem first, to the heavens. There followed the passages I had remembered in my first experience of the Sweat Lodge and of smoking Tsaviaya's pipe. I read them again with wonder that I was now where the stone for his pipehead came from, procuring the stone for mine, which the pipe-maker would soon be fashioning.

"Behold this pipe! Always remember how sacred it is, and treat it as such, for it will take you to the end. . . . With this sacred pipe you will walk upon the earth, for the Earth is sacred. Every step taken upon her should be a prayer. . . . All things of the universe are joined to you who smoke the Pipe, all send their voices to the Great Spirit. When you pray with this Pipe, you pray for and with everything created."

A warning went with the coming of the Pipe.

"Early one morning, very many winters ago, two Lakota were out hunting with their bows and arrows, and as they were standing on a hill looking for game, they saw in the distance something coming towards them in a very strange and wonderful manner. When this mysterious thing came nearer to them, they saw that it was a very beautiful woman, dressed in white buckskin, and bearing a bundle on her back. Now this woman was so good to look at that one of the Lakota had bad intentions and told his friend of his desire, but this good man said that he must not have such thoughts, for surely

this was a wakan woman. The mysterious person was now
very close to the men, and then putting down her bundle, she
asked the one with bad intentions to come over to her. As the
young man approached the mysterious woman, they were
both covered by a great cloud, and soon when it lifted the
sacred woman was standing there, and at her feet was the
man with the bad thoughts who was now nothing but bones,
and terrible snakes were eating him."

Black Elk emphasized that it should not only be taken as an
event in time, but also as an eternal truth. "Any man," he said,
"who is attached to the senses and to the things of this world,
is one who lives in ignorance and is being consumed by the
snakes which represent his own passions."

This is something to be remembered by those who ask for a
pipe. It is true on every path toward the light. We must receive
with joy and use with loving care and detachment everything
the mysterious Wakan One put here for our growth and for our
happiness. We are guests in the House of the Great Spirit, but
while it would be surly and ill-mannered not to appreciate
what is set before us and give thanks for it, nothing has been
given to us for the ego to exploit, to devour, to destroy. If we
have a large ego-beast with us *it* must be carefully controlled;
it does not have the run of the universe, *we* do.

Detachment from the urges of the lower self, with its trans-
ient desires and passions is a prerequisite for travelling the
Way. In other words we must grow in self-control. Swami
Nikhilananda has said of self-control in his book, *Atmabodha,
Self-Knowledge*. "Self-control is the very core of the Vedantic
discipline; without it no progress is possible in spiritual life,
nor any success in meditation. Self-control means the de-
velopment of will power and also the strengthening of the
determinative faculty, which controls all the sense-organs."

An Amerindian holy man advised, "when you arise in the
morning, give thanks for your life and strength. Give thanks
for your food and give thanks for the joy of living. And if you
see no reason for giving thanks, be sure the fault is in yourselves."

"Behold what you see!" the strange woman said to the good
man. "I am coming to your people and wish to talk with your

chief Hehlokecha Najon (Standing Hollow Horn). Return to him and tell him to prepare a large tipi in which he should gather all his people, and make ready for my coming. I wish to tell you something of importance."

What she had to tell and what she brought them was the coming of the Sacred Pipe.

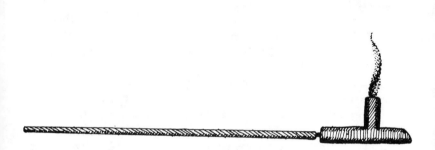

15

When I got back I took the blocks to Power Man, one for him, one for Tsaviaya, one for the Pipemaker, one for my pipe. Then I waited in happy anticipation. What would it look like? Would it be large or small, carved or plain? Would the stem be willow or apple or peach?

I knew that three days must go by before a Medicine Man came to a decision. Perhaps it was the same for Pipemakers. After he decided, I thought it might take a week, or even two, to collect the wood, hollow it out and carve the pipehead and hollow that.

A month went by. Perhaps the Pipemaker was busy, perhaps there were many pipes before mine. I always had a conviction, knowing it was absurd, but still a certainty, that people sprang into activity only when I got in touch them, that they had nothing in the world to do but attend to a message from me instantly, giving it their full attention. It was the same with places. A city stayed as it was when I left it. If I returned it would spring into existence and its citizens go about their lives, in relation to mine. When I left it would be refrozen into a latent state. So now I felt that my Indian friends could have nothing on their minds but my pipe, and were deliberately delaying giving it to me for some reason they expected me to understand.

"Then you wait," Power Man had said. I accepted that, but surely this wait, going into its third month, was too long? Perhaps he was expecting me to make another move. But I knew that one must never ask a Medicine Man twice for anything nor, once asked, refer to the request again until he did. Perhaps he was testing me. If so, it was an efficient test.

I went to the Sweat Lodges, the Ceremonies, and the Doctoring Sweats. Power Man and Tsaviaya ignored me a little more than usual, but the others welcomed me as they always had, with good humored tolerance and amusement. I went on with the routines of daily life, the typing, the chores. I went on seeing those who came to me for advice, for remedies for hurts, those in anguish of mind, bereaved, or beaten down by want and fear to whom a friendly concern, a listening ear, a reminder that 'underneath are the Everlasting Arms' were what they craved and came to receive. There seemed to be more of them during this waiting time. Every day there was somebody at my rickety kitchen table, or walking beside me up the mountain side to the soothing stream.

Day by day my personal interest in receiving the pipe died. When it was no longer in the forefront of my mind, when all the bright speculations about it subsided, when I understood that it was not necessary for me to have a pipe, that I could use the tools I already worked with—herbs, stones, candles, water, color, music, words, things to hand and others I could seek around me; when I knew that I could sit, emptyhanded, in the silence, and become a channel for the healing forces without using *any* tools, then the proper moment, the "when the time is right" of the Indian way, naturally arrived and I received my pipe.

Tsaviaya called me to him before the Sweat.

"Something for you," he said.

On the table was a long white pipestone and beside it the red pipestone head. He took them up in his large gentle hands, fitting them together.

"Peach wood." He touched the carvings on the bowl. "Four for the Four Winds."

"The Four Directions, the Four Old Men?"

He nodded. There were other markings, two sets of notches, one long, one short, with fine points like arrowheads, a fifth point in the center, like a directional sighting mark, and four more indentations like thumb marks, where the pipehead joined the stem. There were light flecks in the stone like little stars. Counting the marks together there were nine in front and four behind, making thirteen. Tsaviaya did not mention these. He held the pipe out, told me to "smudge it good", then bring it to the Sweat Lodge to be blessed.

I took it from him and carried it to the car where I kept a bowl and some sage for blessings, protection, emergencies. Before every trip I smudged the car, going round the outside, under the hood, in the driver's seat, in the body of the truck, a simple precaution which anyone can take. In parts of the country where there is no sage, there are cedar wood, pine needles, sweet grass, and other benevolent, goodsmelling herbs. In the cities incense can be obtained from stores supplying churches, or joss sticks can be bought in many small shops. Sandalwood is one of the best. Incense made with musk should not be used. Most important are the faith and force behind the blessing.

I smudged the pipehead and the pipestone separately, then together, invoking the Four Great Powers, adding two more, Grandfather Sky, Mother Earth, six in all. Suddenly words flowed through me without my mind's direction, words from *The Sacred Pipe*, with adaptations. I realized where they came from later. At the time I only knew that they were right and should be said.

"My Grandfather, Wakan Tanka, you are every-thing. All things belong to you. I have placed your herb upon this fire. Its fragrance belongs to you.

"O Wakan Tanka, you are first and always have been. Behold this pipe newly entrusted to me. The Four Powers and the whole universe will be placed in the bowl of this pipe.

"O you where the sun comes up, who guard the light and who give knowledge. There is a place for you in this pipe.

"O you who control the sacred winds, your breath gives life. There is a place for you in this pipe.

"O you, winged power of the place where the sun goes down. You with your guards are ancient and sacred. There is a place for you in this pipe.

"O you, winged power whence come the strong purifying winds, there is a place for you in this pipe.

"Grandfather Eagle, Wanbli Ganesh, who circle in the highest heavens, you see all things above and upon the earth. Here is this new pipe. Help me to send my voice to Wakan Tanka through it. Help me to use this pipe aright.

"O Unchi and Ina, our Grandmother and Mother Earth, you are sacred. We know that it is from you that our bodies come. Look on this new pipe. There is a place for you in this pipe.

"All things give thanks to you, O Wakan-Tanka, we ask of you because we know that you are the only one, that you have power over all things. May this new pipe entrusted to me be a channel to transmit your healing to the world. O Great Spirit, bless us that the people may live."

It was time to go to the Lodge. I walked slowly, cradling the pipe on my right arm as pipes should be carried, to the line waiting to enter. I stood in my place, shy, looking down, trying not to see the interested glances, nor to feel the little stir round me. When it was my turn to scoop up the sage, I did it awkwardly, with my left hand, and dropped my towel. The woman behind me picked it up and carried it for me, an act of friendship like many others that I, in my clumsiness, received from those whose movements were always graceful and right. As I stooped to go in, Power Man, from his seat near the door, took the pipe from me and I went forward round the circle to my place. He put the pipe on a long strand of sage in front of him.

The good friend next to me gave me the towel, murmuring "I am glad for you." Then the burning rocks were coming in and the Sweat began. It was the same timeless, powerfully charged experience, but when Power Man announced that it was a "Grandfather Sweat", that is a Sweat when everyone gives thanks for blessings received, instead of offering petitions for those to come, I felt that the last right-time condition had been met. I knew, of course, that it wasn't for my joy alone, and that Grandfather Sweats were often given, but I was glad there happened to be one on this day.

The Sweat seemed to me particularly beautiful, harmonious and holy. I hardly noticed the heat. I felt loving companionship in the circle, no barriers of race or skin. Outside it might be awkward again, but here we were safely together in our humanhood.

At the end of the Sweat Power Man passed the pipe to me on its bed of sage and I carried it out into the sunlight.

The Pipe is the Amerindian altar. The bowl is the equivalent of the Chalice of the Holy Grail, or the Chinese Pi—the disk of jade with its central sacred hollow, of cups, craters, cauldrons, holes, and all the rich symbolism attached to them on many levels. But one can get lost in symbolism and wander off into research, instead of experiencing the One Truth behind all symbols and reaching to it, living it in simplicity and joy.

The bowl is a circle with a center, the point within the circle, ancient symbol for the Great Source of All. The circle also represents the zodiac and the zodiacal cycles, the Arthurian Round Table, the Tibetan and Hindu Mandala, and the Amerindian Great Medicine Wheel. It has been written, "To leave the circumference for the centre is equivalent to moving from the exterior to the interior, from form to contemplation, from multiplicity to unity, from space to spacelessness, from time to timelessness. In all symbols expressive of the mystic Center, the intention is to reveal to Man the meaning of the primordial 'paradisal state' and to teach him to identify himself with the supreme principle of the universe."

All these things are in the pipehead as they are also in the heart of a flower, the center of a volcano, the nucleus of a snowflake or the solar plexus—the middle chamber of man's inner temple. It is good to have this knowledge in the background of the mind, confirmation of the Oneness of the great Cosmic blueprint behind all faiths, all religions, all paths to the Light. But at the time of smoking one should lay these thoughts aside and concentrate on becoming a clean and clear channel for the reception and transmission of the Great Spirit's blessing.

The pipestem also has many symbolic meanings, one of the most obvious being the magicians's baton or rod, which must be fashioned of certain woods gathered in a certain way and consecrated to magical uses only. A straight branch of almond, hazel, peach or willow cut before the tree blossomed; cut with a straight sickle in the early dawn was one of the recommended methods of preparation for such a wand. The rod was also hollow like the Chinese Hollow Bamboo, representing the Sage or wise human being after the pith of the lower self had been withdrawn. It referred to the Tao of right living, 'sageliness within, kingliness without'.

Sageliness or wisdom is an inner achievement. Kingliness refers to the ruler who in ancient days was considered divine, who served as the connecting link between Heaven and Earth. This is also the function of the pipestem, to be a two-way line of communication between 'Those Above' and humankind.

16

I hung the Pipe on the west wall of my hut, as I was instructed to do, protected in its frame of sage, until I could make the traditional pipebag for it. This must be made by the person to whom the Pipe has been entrusted. No one else should make it. I have seen men struggling clumsily to sew their pipebags, while their wives, expert workers in buckskin, looked on sympathetically, offering advice but no actual help.

Buckskin is the ideal material for a pipebag, but buckskin nowadays is hard to come by and very expensive. Other forms of leather or cloth are used. The bag must have the right shape, the traditional fringing, and though some bags are richly decorated with beadwork, if they shelter "working pipes", those used for ceremonial and healing purposes, they must have the simplicity of bareness. While I waited to obtain the right material for mine and to learn how to make it, I shrouded it in long strands of sage freshly gathered from the mountain, over a piece of rose colored cloth.

The only west wall available in the hut was in the living room, into which everyone stepped. I had been warned that no one must touch the Pipe but me, but it made an embarrassingly striking "conversation piece" and I found my white friends constantly moved to get up and examine it, to ask curious questions, to stretch out their hands . . .

"No, no," I had to tell them. "You mustn't touch it."

"But what is it?"

Most of them were offended when I said, "Never mind," and changed the subject.

I was complaining about this to Rosella and some of the other women, as we were dressing after the Sweat. A strange look passed through the group.

"It's because you left out an important part," Rosella said solemnly.

"Oh? What didn't I do?"

"You must get a large square of paper. . . ."

"White paper, very white," one of them put in.

"Yes? White paper. How big?"

"About so." She measured with her hands.

"And then you must get black. . . . ."

"Black paint, black ink."

"Black ink? Yes."

"To make special marks."

There was a silence while they looked at me.

"And then you must hang it up under the Pipe."

"But what sort of marks?" I asked, thinking of sign-language or pictographs.

"You must put PLEASE DON'T ASK."

Then everyone laughed, and I laughed too, glad to be teased because I knew it meant they liked me. They had a lot of fun with their token White apple. Once, when I still thought I might be able to learn Paiute, they rehearsed me in a sentence, first one and then another of the women would coach me in it, and hear me repeat it, until they all agreed I had it right. They wouldn't tell me the meaning.

"When the time is right."

After a Sermony, one night, they told me to go over to the group around Power Man and say my sentence, and then Power Man would tell me what it meant.

So I crossed the room, to where the important people stood around the Medicine Man, and when I got their attention, and they turned surprised toward me, I proudly and carefully delivered my sentence. It turned out to be an untranslatable obscenity. It made the evening for everyone but me, and I was not allowed to forget it for many Sermonies.

I disgraced myself at another memorable Sermony. This time there were so many people that we sat in four circles. I was in the front row. We were instructed to change places with the row behind us by sliding backwards, repeating this each time until the front row would be the last row.

Mindful that to them I represented "the whites", I was determined to do everything unobtrusively and right. Sliding on my cushion I started to move back with the others, in the total darkness. Presently I became aware of movement on my left, but none on my right. No one was coming forward past me. Probably, I thought, I hadn't moved far enough back, so I went a little further, and further. Still no one came up on the right, so I slid again.

When the lights went up I was far out in front, among the sacred objects, near Power Man. Bursts of laughter and startled exclamations broke out. Tsaviaya left his place and took me firmly by the ear. With his other hand he pulled me up, pushed me into the front line and sat me down on the bare floor without my cushion.

"You stay *there*," he said, while everyone laughed again.

Later I understood that I should not have been thinking of myself and my part in the Ceremony, but only of the ceremony itself. I also realized that I had been backing away from the *sound*, from the singing and the drumming, instead of from the center where the Power was, and so I had backed into it instead.

The day after I brought the Pipe home I woke with a remembered dream, one of *those*, the more than ordinary dreams. I was on the mountain, in a group of people. They were smoking my pipe. Suddenly I found I didn't have to wait for it to make the circle and return to me. I could smoke without it. Pure white clouds poured from my mouth. I rose and ran, half leaping, half flying, down the mountainside, puffing white blessings as I went, blissfully aware that I *was* the Pipe and always would be.

Words of power and blessing flowed from me. I "talked", I chanted. When I was fully awake and dressed, without waiting for breakfast, I took the Pipe in its covering of sage and went up the mountainside to smoke it for the first time.

Power Man had given me a supply of Indian tobacco, kinni-kin-nick, of herbs, bark and the wild tobacco plant, akin to lobelia. He showed me how to prepare it for myself in the right proportions, "and when you can't get anything else, use Bull Durham."

I filled the pipebowl in the ritual way, trembling a little as I offered it to the Grandfathers, asking for permission to smoke it in the place where I was, asking for Their protection while I smoked, inviting Them to smoke with me, if They would, asking for the prayers in the Pipe and giving thanks for the blessing of having it, and all the blessings of this life.

The match quivered as I lit it and almost went out. I asked the elementals of fire for their help. The tobacco caught. I drew in the first long puff, then I held the pipe up, stem first, turning it slowly in a circle, for the Grandfathers to smoke. I lowered it, drew in the smoke, and raised it again saying "Grandfather Eagle, I send a voice for the prayers in this pipe, for protection and of thanksgiving."

Smoking the pipe, alone, outdoors or in, is a personal, private experience. The omens, the intimations that come, the Presences who make themselves felt, the responses of the natural world, animals who come to be blessed, birds who fly over, dip their wings and return to sing on a nearby bush, flowers opening wider, grasses leaning forward, water in the stream drumming with a new sound and rhythm, these things cannot be discussed without losing force or being taken for coincidence, or even jeered at, which might bring harm on those who jeer. But they can be discovered, felt and understood by those who will sit in commitment and integrity, offering to be a channel for the Grandfathers' work, aspiring to become a grain of tobacco in the Great Spirit's Pipe.

Such commitments with or without a pipe, a stone, a feather, or other focal point, do not go unnoticed by the Grandfathers. Those who share the earth with us make plain their satisfaction. There are signs and tokens to remind us of invisible Watchers, those to whom Saint Paul referred when he said, "Seeing we are encompassed about by so great a cloud of witnesses." Among them I believe there must be many Indians, for sometimes when I smoke in certain places I am overwhelmingly conscious of Indians observing me.

> Chief Sealth (Seattle) said, "Every hillside, every valley, every plain and grove, has been hallowed by some sad or happy event in days long vanished. . . . and at eventide they grow shadowy of returning spirits. And when the last Red Man shall have perished, the memory of my tribe shall have become a myth among white man, these shores will swarm with the invisible dead of my tribe, and when your children's children think themselves alone in the field, the store, the shop, upon the highway, or alone in the silence of the pathless woods, they will not be alone. . . . At night when the streets of your cities and villages are silent and you think them deserted, they will throng with the returning hosts that once filled them and still love this beautiful land. The White Man will never be alone."

The more I smoke the Pipe the more convinced I am of this, but what I wrote in my journal that first smoking day was only: "The cool of the morning, the clouds over the mountain, the blue. Took the Pipe to a hallowed place. Great peace and blessing. Now I understand what Tsaviaya meant when he said that he got all his power, that he 'got everything from the Pipe.' Now I know it's true."

17

After a year of steady practice I learned many things about the Way of the Pipe. I was shown the right way to clean and care for it, the proper way to sit "in a sacred manner", the thorough smudging of myself and of each object to be used such as matches, tobacco, tamping stick—Joshua trees' spikes are good for this and for cleaning the bowl—and I was warned against the insidious temptations of misuse of power.

At first I thought this warning was unnecessary, until I learned how subtle and how real the danger is. People come for help, they ask for some specific thing. Those who smoke the working pipe *know* that they can have what they ask, so at first we ask for that specific thing and feel a little smug when it is granted. Later we begin to understand that the Grandfathers may have better, deeper, wider blessings planned for the asker, waiting for the asking.

We are only channels, transmitters, not originators, "of ourselves we can do nothing." What is required of us is to lift

the asker and his need up to the will of Wankan Tanka, the
Great Spirit, then to keep the channel clear and clean and
open for the descent of the white shaft of healing light that will
rush through us to enfold them.

These are things we must discover for ourselves. When I
tried to ask advice from Tsaviaya he said "I am not to tell you
anything." When I turned to Power Man he said "I cannot tell
you how to use your Pipe, only how to take care of it. What you
do is up to you."

At first, even on the surface, I made many mistakes. When I
took the Pipe up the mountain I sat facing the highest peak,
knowing that there was a great Being there, to whom I was
always drawn. This meant that I was facing west. There was
something a little uncomfortable about this first smoking,
until it dawned on me that I should face the east. I apologized
to the Grandfathers, and after that I sat looking out across the
valley with my back to the mountain range. Then everything
fell into place. The first time that I sat rightly I was startled,
but not frightened, to feel a pressure between my shoulder
blades, like an approving friendly hand, and always when I
smoked in that place, however cold a wind might be blowing,
there was a comforting warmth where the pressure had been.

Gradually the Pipe became an extension of myself, as a
flute becomes to a flautist, or a much-loved, much-used tool to
a craftsman. This is true for any object used in meditation or
healing work. Those who don't have pipes can select a stone,
or some other natural object with which they feel close empathy, and in the course of time and unselfish use of it, can
discover this truth for themselves.

When people come for help, it is good to remind them of the
old saying, "Ask what you will, *and pay for it*, says God."
Another reminder of the level on which the smoking of the Pipe
takes place is the fact that no money may be offered or accepted for it. A small amount of tobacco should be given as part of
the ritual, to serve as a link between the Pipe and the asker.

When people ask me what tobacco I use, I cannot tell them
exactly what there is in the pouch. Basically it is kinni-
kinnick, willow bark, wild Indian tobacco, with Bull Durham,
and other tobacco offered to me. I have to refuse tobacco made
with alcohol or other fermentations. Bull Durham is perhaps

the best for an asker to offer. The little bags cost 12 cents. They used to cost less, tomorrow they may cost more, but even if they rise to a quarter, this is not beyond the means of any. Nor should this offering of tobacco be omitted. It is good for the askers to see the smoke from their own contribution ascending to the Great Spirit. It makes it easier for them to understand that we are all grains of tobacco in the Cosmic Pipe.

In cases of emergency, when the asker has come empty-handed, it is good to point out that there is a supply of excess tobacco given by others, from which we can draw what is needed, and that this can be replaced later. This extra supply is also used to give offerings to the Grandfathers, to bless the places where one smokes and for other purposes. It is good to tell the askers that the tobacco they give links them to the offerings it is used for. I also tell them that once they have smoked the Pipe they will always be included in the blessing I ask on all those who have ever smoked it with me, that they may remember in moments of danger or temptation that there is a network of power, prayer and love to augment their own appeal to the Great Spirit. It also reminds us of the inter-dependence of created things.

"For so the whole round earth is every way
Bound by gold chains—(pure ascending smoke)
—about the feet of God."

Tennyson, *Idylls of the King*

Over the years I have smoked on mountains, in national forests, besides lakes, by river banks, in deserts, off high-ways, in cities, even in motel rooms, always blessing the places, and leaving an offering for the Grandfather in charge of that region. A map of all these linked places across the continent would be interesting. I think it might show a significant geometric pattern.

Once I remember smoking with a family on the fire-escape back porch of an apartment building in Louisville, Kentucky, all among the garbage cans. It was the only place available for any privacy. As we smoked, people were passing, laughing and talking below. Suddenly a woman looked up and saw us. There was a startled exclamation from the man sitting next to me. He got up and plunged down the staircase to the street. It turned out afterward that this woman was a lost-sight-of friend for whom he had been praying a moment before.

No one sees us who is not supposed to see us. I have been smoking beside a stream and had fishermen pass within a few feet, unseeing. I have had people arrive just after the pipe is put away, while the sage is still burning in front of me, and say such things as "what a good idea! It must keep the mosquitos away."

I believe that if it were necessary to smoke in Grand Central Station, I could sit down in the center of the crowd and not be seen. But it would have to be necessary. I would have to be told by the Grandfathers to do it. It could not be to show off on my own.

Once in Hopi country I could not find a secluded place to smoke. It was flat sandy territory, where everything was visible for many miles. I saw a slight dip in the sand, and went up a little track to it. Crouching low with my companion I started the ritual. Presently she murmured "Oh oh, we have visitors." A truck had turned off the road and followed us. I asked the Grandfathers for protection and went on smoking. When it got to about fifty feet from us, it stopped, turned and went away.

Several times Power Man sent me to ask for a blessing and give offerings in special places. Once he sent me to Pyramid Lake in Nevada, because, he said, "the people there are not taking care of their lake in a sacred manner."

When I finally found a place free of tourists and secluded from interruptions, as well as I could judge, a golden eagle circled low above me as I smoked, and as I left the place, another eagle, a big black one, flew straight down the highway toward my car, and then turned and conducted me for a mile along my way.

It is not unusual for eagles, other birds, and animals to take part in the smoking, and though this is not necessary to assure us that the Grandfathers know what we are doing, and are with us when we smoke, it is a lovely bonus. For example, in the summer of 1976 I was sent to Georgia to help a serious situation in a community there. On the second day as I sat down with my pipe, a dog appeared and sat beside me. When

I had finished he got up and trotted off. Every day after that he appeared, for his blessing and though I smoked at different times and places he always knew where and when to find me. After a week of this he appeared one day with three cats following him. He sat on one side, the cats on the other, all perfectly still until the ceremony was over, when they went away. It got to be a regular procession, up the hill in single file, to the amusement of the people who watched it. Presently those people, too, were coming to take part in the smoking. Then the dog still sat beside me, but the cats divided themselves among the people, setting a dignified example of alert attention and stillness.

It is more startling perhaps when the wild ones come. In certain places it is the birds, in others the four-footed, and in some, bees and other insects. This is an indication of who the Grandfathers of that region may be. Some Grandfathers are four-footed, and then the pipe has a certain quality of, not heaviness, but solidarity. Some are winged and the pipe is lighter, more volatile. In one place in California, the Grandfather is a Golden Bee, who appears first, and is followed by other bees and stinging, humming insects. This used to startle me at first, I was disturbed when they came very near and even alighted on my hands and face. I used to be allergic to bee-sting, and had to go to the hospital if I was stung more than once.

I learned to control, then to banish fear, to welcome bees and insects, bless them, speak to them gently, asking them to withdraw a little but not to go away. This they did, circling at a distance, and at the most sacred parts of the ceremony, alighting on branches or rocks and keeping still. After awhile I grew so used to their coming to that place that I think I would have missed them if they hadn't arrived to receive the blessing of the Pipe and take it back to their communities.

When we pass through different regions it is courteous to ask permission from the Grandfather of that countryside to smoke, and to ask for protection while smoking, also to offer the pipe to the Grandfather so that if he chooses to he may smoke it first.

Once in bear country I heard heavy footsteps in the underbrush. I continued to smoke but my heart beat faster and my breath came unevenly. The footsteps stopped when they were very near, behind a clump of bushes directly opposite. I felt, I *knew*, Grandfather Bear was standing there. I tried to control excitement tinged with fear. A long moment passed. Then slowly, on a boulder facing me, a face began to emerge, from within the rock, but also as though it were being drawn or etched there, like a pictograph. It was the face of a bear, gravely regarding me, muzzle lifted as though to sniff. My companion saw it too, though she told me later she had not heard the approaching footsteps.

I smoked on, asking for extra blessings on the region, for the Grandfather, the Deva and the nature-spirits. The head on the rock began to fade, till with the last long puffs it was gone. The underbrush crackled, there was the sound of a heavy animal moving away. This time my companion heard it. We felt exhilarated, accepted, privileged, in harmony with the Grandfather and with Mother Earth. All that day we were conscious of being watched, of awareness in the forest on both sides of the road, until we travelled out of that territory into the domain of another Grandfather, this time winged.

Next day we found a place, around high noon, where the Nez Perce held a council for peace, according to the historical marker by the roadside. We climbed a barb-wire fence behind the marker and went a little way to the left behind trees and bushes. Here D., my companion, found a suitable rock and here we sat down to smoke. I asked the Grandfathers of that region for permission to smoke there, for protection while we smoked, and for a blessing on the Sweat Lodge and the people at home. I said who we were, where from, what we were doing, and the missions we were travelling towards.

As I smoked, the sound of a big bird directly above us came, very strange and clear, rather like the whistle of the eagle-bone flutes in some of the ceremonies. We could see no bird in the sky, and we could see the sky for several miles. It stayed there, unseen, above us, whistling. A goose, we thought. Later we discovered that Chief White Bird, whose region we had just come through, was named for white wild goose. Certainly the bird sounded like a goose. As we left there were two eagles soaring above us, and we were both filled with satisfaction and peace which lasted for a long time.

Soon after this we came to an Indian reservation, Nez Perce, with a museum, and we stopped there. This was Chief Joseph's tribe, and also Chief White Bird's. I asked two Indian women at the Museum for some information about Chief White Bird and got a harsh brush-off, which saddened us, for we were still starry-high with the sound of the great Bird. We had hoped they would be perceptive and realize that we were pipe-people, or at any rate bridge-builders. But these were embittered, white-hating Indians, such as we were to meet with later in full force in our own part of the country. They took out their rancor on us and we got out of there, and drove on pensively.

The next day it was hard to find a place to smoke, this time because of white hostility. The land was fenced in on both sides of us for many miles. No Trespassing signs were on every gate and on many trees. It is a normal experience to travel all day without finding a "right-feeling" place to smoke. I sometimes wonder what would happen if we rode up to the door of a ranch and said "We have come to bless the land. May we have your permission to smoke the sacred Pipe beneath those trees?" But I have never risked it, and that is why we sometimes see the Eagle or his messengers, the crows, circling above a special place, pointing to it, asking us to come there, and we are unable to comply, shut out by No Trespassing signs, or the even ruder "Keep OUT! This means YOU!" nailed to some sad tree.

For a long time we drove in the territory of Grandfather White Bird between the man-made barriers until, when it was getting rather late we saw a little track, ungated, unfenced, leading off to the left. We followed it hopefully, but here the land was flat and we were in plain sight of the main highway. Presently we saw a dip in the land and some trees which seemed to promise cover. We turned off the track to a rougher one and drove towards them hopefully. They sheltered a small pond, fringed with tall reeds and bushes. As we got out of the car the sky was filled with geese, whirling and circling above our heads, honking and crying. There was one large group then a smaller one, of seven, and another of six, with one always flying ahead, in charge, it seemed, not only of that group but of the whole community. They were not Canada geese, because they were all white. We wondered, snow geese perhaps? But these are rare.

Suddenly they all shot down into the pond, and we went forward to smoke in the clump of trees. It was a long hard pipe. We had many sick and troubled people in it, and there was this new territory to bless. As we finished a small bird came and sat on a branch, talking excitedly. I whistled back. When I stopped, D. said "Where have they gone? Did you hear them leave?"

There was not a trace of geese in all that wide sky, nor in the pond. They had gone as they had come, as eagles go into the sun, and as soundlessly, no splash of water, no whirr of wings, no honk. It seemed impossible. "I wasn't *that* concentrated," D. said. "Were you? I heard a lot of other things, a car on the road, and a tractor and the wind."

While we still looked around, my tobacco can, quite a heavy one, rose off the rock on which it was sitting, tipped over sideways, and the lid came off. It was hard to pry open, normally, but perhaps I had not closed it properly after filling the Pipe. D. gaped and muttered "Let's get out of here!" but I was already talking to the nature-spirits soothingly. After smoking, especially in new territories, the Grandfathers expect an offering of tobacco, which the "little men of the mountains" and the other gnomes and elementals especially enjoy. Here the little people were impatient for their offering, which I was slow in giving, since I was still searching the sky for geese. I apologized that they had had to help themselves, went over to pick up the can and scatter more grains on the ground and some in the pond. Offerings of consecrated tobacco grains placed in waterfalls, rivers, and streams purify the flow of water from the source to the furthest outlet, and the land which this water reaches; in ponds and lakes the effect is the same, though here there is no rushing forward on the foam, it is slower, more stately, a circular motion round the edges, toward the center, and back to the circumference. The offering is made to the water spirits, who take charge of it. On land the earth spirits distribute the blessing, and one more corner is cleaner, lighter.

I explained this to D. to whom some of the ways of the Pipe path were still strange, and I told her what I remembered about the goose. Hansa was the sacred goose, swan or duck of Brahma, on which he rides. It was sent by Siva and Vishnu to awaken him to creative work when he slept. The eggs of the Hansa, in Sanskrit literature are said to be full of ambrosia. They swim on the waters, and the Hansa is said to be "drunk with love."

"They certainly acted that way this time," D. said.

Hansa is the goose that lays the golden eggs, (sun and moon) and also a messenger of love. The goose stands for conjugal fidelity. In Egypt Seb (the Earth) is a goose, "the great cackler" who lays the gold egg, the sun. In mythology the goose is often confused with the swan, the emblem of white and snow, clouds and mystery. The goose is also an emblem of Frey and the Swan of Freya. Swans and geese were choristers of Apollo in spring.

These wild white geese from Canada, or from further north, or even perhaps from the Spirit Land, were messengers from the Great Spirit. They lifted our spirits into joy and gratitude for the magic and wonder of the universe, and we spoke of them much as we drove on the last laps of our journey homeward.

It is the custom on the first Sweat of the month to bring the Pipes to the Lodge to be blessed. We sit beneath our pipebags, fastened behind us. It is a strange feeling to have the Pipe behind instead of in front, with the vibrations of power coming through the shoulders and the sacroiliac, instead of upwards towards the heart and throat. The effect of the vibrations from each suspended Pipe, adding to the power generated in the lodge makes this first Sweat of the month different from all others.

It is especially so after an absence on a travelling mission when we relate what we can of what we have done and experienced to our brothers and sisters whose prayers have followed and helped to protect us. It is in these exchanges that the sturdiest bridges of understanding are built.

There is more to tell about the Pipe, but these are things we must discover and experience for ourselves. As Tsaviaya and

Power Man said no one can tell us what to do with our Pipes, our stones, our feathers, or whatever else we use for sacred objects. These are individual procedures, unique to each of us. Some things are constant and can be taught and learned from others, e.g. the proper care of what we use for meditation, prayer and healing, the respect and protection with which we surround them, and above all never to use them, or anything the Great Spirit gives us, for selfish ends. If we are ambitious for ourselves, for personal power or prestige, our contact with the Grandfathers will be blocked, the power in our Pipes go away, and we will no more be clear channels for the healing forces of the Great White Light.

So much we can be taught. The rest, as Power Man, or any true Medicine Man or teacher will tell us, "is up to us."

18

When I had had the Pipe for about a year, the time was right for me to go into my first fast. I went to Power Man's reservation in Wyoming. I went alone, after a send-off Sweat in Tsaviaya's Sweat Lodge. I had no family to take care of me, but Power Man's wife offered to be my family, to "stand behind" me during the fast. This was an honor and also a comfort, although I didn't know then all that it would entail for both of us.

It was a two-day drive, during which I had time to think and to prepare myself as I had been doing for several weeks. It is the custom for the person fasting to provide the food for the Medicine Man, his family, and those who come to the Sweats and Ceremonies before and after the "putting in."

The car was loaded with provisions and "give-aways" to be distributed, blankets, clothing, household goods, tobacco, hardware, beads, something for everyone who would come to help the fast and to receive the special blessing poured out at that time. Give-aways must always be new, so fasting is an expensive sacrifice, which people have to save for, often for years. As soon as I knew that I was going to fast I began to save and buy at sales, and ask my friends to contribute little gifts. The friend who helped me to get to Minnesota gave me $100 toward gas and food. Without that I could not have managed. Also Power Man chose a time when three men were "going in", and we could share the expenses.

Even so it was a sacrifice for all of us, as a fast should be. I knew the more important parts took place on higher levels, but I liked the symbolism of the fasting ones providing the food for others, who should remember them as they ate, taking care to eat and drink for them, so that they would not suffer too much from hunger or thirst, but be set free from these to fast in other deeper ways.

I was to "go in" for two nights, the usual first-time fast. The nights were the important part. During the days I might rest, even doze a little in my fasting lodge, but during the nights I must not sleep. During the fast nothing must pass my lips, no food, no water, not even a piece of sage. In fact I must not touch my mouth with anything except the pipe. I must sit erect on the tule reeds, facing the east, holding the Pipe which would be ceremonially "stuffed" by the Medicine Man. I must chant and pray aloud and talk to the spirits who would come in to check on my sincerity and all that happened in the fasting lodge. Fast Lodges are small individual shelters built by the Medicine man and those who will use them, and taken down after the fast is over.

So much I knew theoretically. The actual participation was as far beyond theoretical knowledge as watching a swan-dive is from taking off from the springboard. Nor did the pilgrimage towards it prepare me for the total experience.

The journey was part of the fasting. My diary for June 14th 1970 says, in part:

Got up early and stole away to "wrench out" my sweat clothes and get a purifying bath in the hot springs. Then, carelessly, after the good hour, got stuck on a rock and couldn't get the car off. I tried everything and finally walked

two miles to the nearest house, uncertain of what I might find.
I roused a young man from his Sunday sleep. He came back
with me, balanced the car off the rock, and I was able to go on,
a long lonely grim journey, with the generator warning light
coming on in a desolate place. I drove in some anxiety, but
thinking of the beauty of the planet, the fast that is to be and
the strangeness of things.

After some hours I reached a service station and had a
battery quick-charge, but driving through long deserted roads
with the red light on is a strain. I put the problem up to the
Grandfathers, determined to arrive at the fast, if I had to
hitch-hike, walk or crawl. The Grandfathers took care of it.
Eventually I reached Salt Lake City, and found that the
generator fan had broken. That was all. After thinking that I
wouldn't get to the reservation today I arrived in the late
afternoon and was warmly welcomed. There was a large
camp. I parked where I was told, opposite a teepee, facing an
open meadow, and settled down to community life. Fortunately I do know Power Man and his wife, and a few of the
others. Those who don't know me will have to accept me, I
suppose, since we all sweat together. I wish I had outgoing
warmth and charm of manner. I get to crouching and frowning
as I did in _____ when I was in that exclusive society. I don't
quite fit in completely anywhere, but somewhat everywhere.

Tuesday, June 16th, 1970.

A long, rather strainful day, living in the public eye. But the
Sweat in the evening was wonderful. It was a Doctoring
Sweat, for a man with cancer of the lung, and a check-up for
Power Man's wife. I hope nothing is wrong with her. She is too
valuable.

Wednesday, June 17th.

Woke at 2. a.m. and decided to smoke my Pipe to get rid of
some of the hostilities and strains I feel with the group next
door, particularly. And was blessed and freed. Then breakfast
with Power Man and family, and after that I took off looking for
a place to wash my Sweat clothes. I found it by a bend in the
river. Had it all to myself, and did pouches, and wrote this. I
will come often to this bend in the river while I am here.

This evening the putting-in Sweat. Four rounds, no openings, and yet it was not too unbearably hot. Later, under the

full moon, conducted the three to their fasting places. They are going in for four nights. Power Man sealed them in, while we circumambulated, sang to them, touched the doorposts and left them to their lonely vigils. A remarkable and strange experience. We went in single file across the fields, in silence, a long procession, wrapped in blankets and shawls. Cars were passing on the distant highway, but here it might have been hundreds of years ago.

Eventually we reached the place where there were three small wickiups—rough shelters of boughs and reeds—with openings to the east, about a hundred feet apart. Each man stood at the door of his lodge, waiting to be sealed within it. The ritual was long and very moving. The ceremonial sealing of the openings, with tobacco flags and other things, was final and complete. The openings must be found untampered with in the dawn, when Power Man goes to let the fasters out, for awhile. Then they must go back into the lodges for the day, and be sealed up again in them at night.

The families and friends whispered words of faith and encouragement to each man through the sealed doorways, then we left in single file again across the fields. It was rough walking in the darkness lit only by moonlight. Someone fell in a ditch and was dragged out of it, in silence. I stumbled and lost a shoe, but did not dare get out of line to look for it. Someone behind me picked it up and passed it on to me.

Thursday June 18th.

I "went behind the blanket", needing to be alone, and took off to the place I found yesterday, by the river. Today and part of yesterday I have wanted to cry, and at times have actually done so. This is very unlike me, the more so that I am conscious of serenity and even joy beneath the tears. This is Cosmic grief, perhaps, part of the fast.

"Drop, drop, slow tears. . . . " I am already fasting from many things:— water running conveniently, clean and private toilets, a more comfortable bed than the cluttered back of the car, though it serves faithfully and I sleep well in it; peace from constant shouts and noise, peace from crowd exchanges and loud laughter at elementary jokes, also, on the mental plane, I am fasting from books, music and conversation. All these are tests.

Friday, June 19th.

By the river again. I took a small stone from the place where I sit and put an offering of sage there instead. It is an ordinary pebble but the vibrations of the river are in it.

This is the day I too "go in." I am fasting for the vow I made that I would fast, also for A . . . and B. . . . their health and their paths toward the Light, and, the main purpose of this fast, to become a dedicated healer, walking the Beauty Way.

Later, a terribly hot Sweat, but I got through it somehow, and now I'm waiting beside my car to be told what to do. The three men are fasting on the horizon. The breeze is soft and cold about my face, but I am already thirsty. The others are eating and drinking the meal I supplied. I don't know whether I was supposed to go there and eat with them, but to be safe I am not going, which will make my fast more complete, if I should have eaten, and save my face, if I shouldn't.

All my life I have been anxious about right timing, and uncertain about what I was supposed to do. Group living like this throws me, waiting throws me, which is why it is a bit unnerving tonight, like waiting at an airport for a plane, or a bus station for a bus.

One wants to be in one's seat and settled for the journey. These preliminaries to the fast are good for me, no doubt, but I am tempted to think I have been forgotten, left behind, a childhood trauma. Also I dislike not being told things, or told contradictory things, all the small niggling tests to teach us to "take the elevator" and the long view from above.

It turned out that I was expected to eat with the others, but as usual "It's up to you", up to me, they thought, and respected my absence. Power Man's wife had said they would put me in "directly after Sweat", a slip of the tongue for "directly after Ceremonies." The time came at last. I was taken to my fast lodge, not across the fields where the men were, but to a small Sweat Lodge, behind the big one. Many came to see me put in, shake my hands and wish me success. Some asked me to pray for them, all said they would pray for me. I felt a surge of love for these, the people, for whom I would be fasting, whom I would represent.

I stood with my Pipe, facing the East. Power Man said a long melodic prayer in ancient Arapaho, then he led me in, smudged the place, blessed me with sweet grass, and backed slowly out. His wife had folded my fast-blanket on the reeds. I sat down on it and they sealed me in.

The darkness was sudden, complete, startling. I began to pray aloud, self-consciously at first, knowing that I was being overheard by the silent group outside. I knew, from having taken part in the sealing in of the three men, what must be happening outside, how they were listening, and would be for awhile, before they left me to the testing of the Spirits.

The first hours of a fast are frightening, lonely, solemn. They are like internment, the internment of the Master, even to the signs of grief and distress. Suddenly, overwhelmingly, I began to sob, crying for the desperation in the world. I cried for fear, for misery, for pain on all the layered planes of life, mineral, vegetable, animal, human, and out beyond them into space. I cried for injustices, wrongs, pollutions, woundings of Mother Earth and the sentient lives on her. I cried and could not stop, but I knew that it was not for self-pity. It was a generous sorrow, a Cosmic, cleansing sorrow, welling up from tremendous unknown depths above a core of serenity that did not change.

I do not know how long I cried on that first night. Time is not, in the fast. Presently there were little flashing lights like those I had seen in Sweat Lodges. Gradually I became aware of a Gray Shape, dimly outlined in the blackness, seated with its back to the East, bowed forward, seeming to listen attentively, impassively, to my sobbing. My crying died away in a few last shuddering sobs. I began to "talk" to this featureless Someone, sitting in judgment upon me, and through me upon all of us, for I knew that in that place, at that time, I represented the people.

Words died as weeping had. I sat in silence, holding my Pipe. A great weariness came upon me, worse than hunger or thirst. My body longed to surrender, to lie down, to sleep, but that would be to fail in the trust, in the vigil. I knew that though I was alone, in the universe, cut off completely from all life as I had known it, somewhere out there other sentient beings depended upon me to be true, to endure this fast to the end. I started to pray aloud, hard.

"Now you may smoke Pipe," a grave voice in my head said to me. I looked toward the Shape. It had gone. There was nothing but "darkness visible" in this tomb where I was sitting. I groped for the two matches I had been given, struck one of them against my thumb and lit the Pipe. I was so exhausted that I forgot to remove the stopper of sage Power Man had sealed it with, and smoked that too. Smoking sage is strong and purifying. Smoking in darkness is a strangely limited experience. Apparently several senses are involved in the total act, besides the sense of smell, sense of taste, etc. To fast from one of these destroys the balance of the whole involvement. Sight, I discovered is essentially important.

Still it was a comfort to talk through the Pipe to the Grandfathers, to feel familiar contact as a dedicated Pipe Woman, rededicated through this voluntary sacrifice. Slow puff after slow puff went to the blessing of this one, that one, to the earth, the water, the air, the fire, the Grandfathers, the Sweat Lodges, the Fasting Lodges, the men undergoing initiation in them, to Power Man and his family, to all the red-skinned peoples, and to me. The last puff went up, the Pipe grew cold, I cleaned it and put it across my lap and sat in meditation.

When a cock crew I knew that dawn was near. The flap of the opening went up. Power Man's wife, going silently, with her special grace, past the oblong of gray light, unsealed me for the day. I staggered up, and stepped outside. In haste and crudity, instead of praying to the Sun as the representative of the Great Spirit, as I should have done, I made a bee line for the toilet.

A young Indian was coming out of it. He held the door open for me, with respect for the fasting victim, and I swept inside. It was somehow regal and touching. The government gave the Indians no plumbing, but with what dignity they use their outhouses!

Then I went back to a long hot day of deprivation, of strident noise. The men in the distance were in quietude, but my fast lodge was in the center of the camp. Heat, discomfort, thirst, mosquitos, tear-blubbered face, tangled hair, and a feeling of sodden dirt, were all part of the fast, the physical part.

Through the open flap I could see the nearby Sweat Lodge and beyond it alfalfa fields. After many dragging hours I saw the fire built and lit to heat the rocks, and finally the people going in to sweat. I listened to the familiar chants and joined in mentally.

Power Man and his son came at dusk to seal me in for the second night. Once more they smudged me with sage and sweet grass, smudged the lodge, the bedroll, then Power Man stuffed the Pipe and smudged it. At the opening he turned and broke from silence to say a long Arapaho prayer, then he was gone, the flap fell into place, was tightly secured and I was again in total blackness, and again afraid. But this time fear passed quickly. It was calmer in the fast lodge and in my spirit. Sadness was still about me but I did not weep.

I prayed aloud, remembering the three men fasting in deeper, more discomfort than I, for double the nights. I renewed my vows and sat in meditation with the Pipe across my knees.

White Eagle has said "At the beginning of your creation you lay in the heart of the Logos. All truth lies in that simple and central thought. When you were breathed forth into incarnation, when you departed from the heart of the Great Spirit and found you possessed free will, you used it like a wayward child. As a result you fell into the mire of suffering; there indeed you suffered, and are still suffering.

" If you would progress to the heart of the mysteries of the Cosmos, your way lies through meditation upon and realization of the still, small voice, the Great Spirit within; for all the mysteries of eternity lie within your heart."

His teachings now came back to me in the darkness and the solitude of this interment, for in truth the fast lodge is a tomb. The ceremonies of the sealing in are like the ceremonies of a funeral. Those outside, who bury us with careful hands and prescribed ritual may love and pray for us, but they cannot reach us. We cannot be reached by anything from the outer world. Only those from the Spirit World, may enter here. Their emissaries are everywhere. In place of the great gray judging One who had come the night before, there were other, smaller, gentler presences. I felt the brush of wings, the touch of hands, and once a scrabbling on my head as though some bird were probing with his beak, a yellow beak, I thought it was, of a big white bird.

"Grandfather Eagle," I prayed, "place your wisdom in my head," at which the scrabbling changed to three sharp blows, the fast lodge filled with lavender light, and then I think I may have left in trance. I came back to the darkness, pressing upon me like the folds of a living cloak, which I felt might suffocate my human overcoat, so I lit and smoked the Pipe, and when I finished, almost at once the dawn was there.

Power Man's wife threw up the flap. She beckoned to me to step outside. I did and prayed to the sun as the representative of the Great Spirit. Then I went to the outhouse. When I came back she handed me clean sweat clothes. I shed my fasting blanket, put them on, and waited.

Suddenly, past the opening, in the faint light of dawn and the fire, came a swift, awe-inspiring procession of tall shrouded figures in single file, and behind them helpers carrying their gear. Power Man summoned me sharply to follow and take my place with them outside the Sweat Lodge. I did so, feeling self-conscious, especially before the women, scanning my face for signs that I had fasted well or ill.

We went into the Sweat, the three men first, then I, then Power Man's wife, and after that the rest of the people, crowding close. It was a hot, gruelling sweat. We learned that one man had nearly failed and another was not sure if he had done everything right. Two of them were weeping. The man next to me was calm and controlled. He later became a Medicine Man, and I often attended his Sweat Lodge. There is a lifelong bond between fasting people.

We were told to speak, I too, thanking the Grandfathers and those who had sustained us with their prayers, and to tell in short general terms what we experienced. After a long silence Power Man said "The Grandfathers say all has been done right."

There were sobs of relief and hy-ehs all round. The Sweat continued. I managed pretty well until the last round, when I fell over sideways onto the lap of Power Man's wife. She pushed me up, strengthening me, she was my family, "standing behind me", to receive the water, ceremonially handed to the fasting ones. It came to me first. She murmured to drink a little, only a little, and throw the rest upon the fire. It was passed to the others, who did the same, with gestures and prayers I should have made. Then the Pipe and the long smoking, the long wait while all the people smoked, then the four of us fasting ones, then Power Man, then OUT, into the sunshine, into the shower, to the car for clean clothes, and to a big meal outside under the trees. I was careful not to take much, and later I drove to the bend of the river and spent the day there resting. I was very hot, and my overcoat weak and feverish, but I was calm and contented, my first fast over.

My diary says: "Tonight there was a powwow. I went to some of it. Tomorrow more sweat and the third night of ceremonies. Tuesday should be the last and after that departure, with so much to ponder and assess."

As always there is an immediate swoop down after every stumbling step upward. I was accosted by an Indian in my favorite place by the river. He drove up in a car and at first I didn't know what he wanted being still full of my fast and holy experiences. I went towards the car, because he spoke so softly that I didn't hear him.

"Catch anything?"

I said "No. I haven't been fishing. Others may have."

"Aren't you going to fish?"

"No. I haven't a pole."

"*You* don't need a pole."

And then his leer told me what he was after.

"Where you from?"

I said "Fasting." and turned my back and walked away, cross with myself for being so naive, but I am obviously an old, white-haired lady, which should be protection enough. After awhile the car purred slowly away, leaving me deflated and a little put out with the world. This was not, for once, *white* evil. I had been idealizing Indians too much, also their women do not go to riverbends alone."

During the year that followed I thought much about initiation, fasting and the vision-quest. As usual, in this sort of journey it is only after we embark on the new way that the meaning of what we have done and are doing comes to us. In going to my first Sweat Lodge I had started on a path of transmutation. In making the first fast I was entering a process of further evolution. Slowly I realized that I was going on the vision-quest, or at least that I had taken a physical step toward the preparation for it, bringing to concrete form what was already true on other planes.

The Indian fast goes beyond the personal concept of sacrifice. He does not fast only for himself. He fasts for his family, his tribe, his land, his world. Instinctively I did not fast only on my behalf. I fasted as well as I could for all sentient life. My first two-night fast was a small step on the threshold of fasting. Even that much, persevered into the best of my ability, brought me an increase of insight and of power in the Pipe. Later I would enter greater heights and depths of the experience.

19

A year later I went again to Wyoming for the three-night fast, a more important and impressive occasion than the first. This time I travelled with three Paiute friends, who had been with me from my first going in to Tsaviaya's Sweat. They were a married couple and an older woman, a tribal "elder". They had agreed to be my family and "stand behind me."

June 6th 1971

After a farewell Sweat, Eagle Man gave me some last instructions and a little carving of a praying man, made of sacred Pipestone, to go with me and act as a point of contact with him and the Sweat Lodge. We got under way at dawn, and drove until the night, stopping only for food and to change drivers. At one stop a mocking bird came to a fencepost beside us and "talked" urgently. P. reminded us that the Mockingbird understands and speaks Arapaho, which none of us did, so we could not understand the message, except that it was obviously one of interest and goodwill.

We camped for the night by a man-made lake in very white territory. The next day we drove on, arriving at the reservation in the late afternoon. Power Man, P. and others set up our shelter, and soon our family camp was in swing. P. dug the fire hole, H. took charge of the cooking, stringing up deer meat to dry on poles, and getting out her baskets for preparing grain. We are to "live off the land and eat Indian", except for my going-in meal, a mixture of white and red foods, and my coming-out feast which will be glorious! The Californian contingent is determined to do itself proud. I am paying for the food, H. and L. preparing it, and P. attending to the fire.

There are no give-aways except for my fasting blanket and the presents I have brought for Power Man and his family. I don't know why this is , except that the expenses for the food are great and perhaps they think that is enough. My fasting lodge is all set up. It is further off this time, more appropriate to a three-night fast.

This evening, as we sat in our shelter, made festive by gaily colored hangings, quilts and throws, people came to visit us, to shake my hand and wish me well. Some of them were people I knew from the last visit and some of them were strangers. A young mother and I sat talking in a corner, when from her camp came a shout "Time to put the baby to bed!" She shouted back, "Get out the sage!" and after a few more exchanges, rose and strolled away, to "smudge" her baby before settling him for the night. Indian babies whose parents live in the traditional way smudge their babies on waking and the last thing at night. I wish everyone did.

Tuesday June 8th

A long, hot, tiring day, mostly chatter, and I was hoping for Sweats and spiritual things, but it is always this way and somehow part of it, as I should have remembered. Other things are good—the place, the sky, a large horizon, not hemmed in by mountains as we are at home, the camp—and I have to keep telling myself that I am camping with three Paiutes, who look on me as one of them, and that I am being slowly readied to go through a three-night fast in the Arapaho way and that I do believe this fast will be an upward turning point.

Wednesday, June 9th.

Woke to soft Paiute laughter and preparations for breakfast. Later I watched H. dealing with three prairie pups, singeing and roasting them for tonight. I do not dare to enquire or look too closely into the contents of the big cooking pot, but eat and give thanks for what is set before me. L. comes at intervals to make me drink large glasses of tomato juice. "Make you less thirsty when you go in," she says. We laugh and tease each other.

This evening the first Sweat Lodge. Some Canadian Indians have arrived from British Columbia. The two Canadian men use their pipes differently from ours, and they are made of a black pipe-stone. The Sweat went very well for me. Grandfather Eagle came. Later the big meal was rather difficult. There were some hostile vibrations, especially from the Canadians, who are political Indians and hate the whites. Power Man's wife went out of her way to tell them that I was fasting and had already fasted and that I had a pipe, but it made little difference, and I was sorry to be an embarrassment to her. The feeling of being different and disapproved of by society seems to be a part of the fast.

Thursday, June 10th.

I woke this morning at four and smoked my Pipe while the camp was asleep. The smoke went up through the little vent on top of the camper. If anyone had seen it they would have thought I was on fire. Tomorrow I go in. Tonight S. and O. go in. Their families are busy cooking for the going-in meal, and there is much intervisiting between the camps. L. said I must go to the camps too, I might leave out the Canadians, but must wish S. and O. well, and visit some of the others. I did so, bracing myself for the obviously reluctant-to-accept, almost hostile vibes.

Later we took the two men across the fields in silent procession. They were ritually fastened in, blessed, and we touched the door frames, and chanted. Then we left them to their testing, and came back. Some of the people had never taken part in a "putting-in" before. I had, once, but it was as startling and impressive as if I had never seen it. So it was done hundreds, perhaps thousands of years ago and so, for a few, it is still done today.

Friday, June 11th.

Today was my turn. First the Sweat, then the last meal, which L. and H. had prepared all day. They did us proud! Even the Canadian Indians were impressed and the nice wife of one of them said "What a beautiful table!"

After the meal we sat around, under some strain, and I was ready to go in, when there was a flurry and an alarm. S. could not make it. After one night he was in too much pain and had to be taken out. In fact he had already burst out of his fast-lodge. So I was delayed while they went to get him. Poor man, it is better not to take on too much, and when you are under heavy medication as it turns out he is, not to try it at all.

Eventually they put me in, in due form, with a procession and singing. Everyone shook my hand and wished me well. Power Man smudged me and the Fast Lodge, said his Arapaho putting-in prayer, and I was left alone in the darkness of the first night.

It was not like the first night of my first fast. I did not feel the need or obligation to weep. It was a second symbolical journey, on a higher, more serene level, through quieter regions of the inner worlds.

On this plane it was a test of endurance, of trust, of intent. I sat upright on the nubbly reeds, praying aloud, self consciously, inspite of all my efforts to banish this-plane ego, "talking" to Wakan-Tanka, to the Grandfathers, conscious of listeners outside the Fast Lodge, and of shrouded figures inside, in a circle round me. Once my head dropped over the Pipe and I was beginning to doze, when a hand slapped my cheek. I apologized to the Grandfathers and to this Guardian Spirit, and after that I kept my eyes open to the blackness, warring against sleep. Hunger and thirst were not a difficulty yet.

I felt I was on duty, a sentry, not Vaughan's sentry, standing outside the gates of a Celestial City.

"My soul there is a country
Far beyond the stars,
Where stands a winged sentry,
All skillful in the wars."

Henry Vaughan, *Peace*

I could not be that winged one. Here in this small suffocating shelter I could not stand, nor physically see. I could only crouch in commitment, with a sharpened awareness of other senses. I was a sentry in no-man's land, for the lost, the lonely, those who think they stumble in perpetual night.

Voices of those who preceded me rolled through my mind:

"Keep watch. . . ."

"Be vigilant . . ."

"Grandfather, behold me. I give to you these offerings that my people may live."

"We who represent all the people offer ourselves to You that we may live. . . ."

"Wakan Tanka helps those who cry to Him with a pure heart."

Serenity seemed to be a quality of this first night of the second fast, but chiefly the keynote was vigilance.

"It needs but little to overthrow and destroy everything. Keep watch!"

"It is no trifle you have in keeping. Keep watch!"

The voices left me. The lower mind's interference left me. I sank or rose deeper into silence, but it was a speaking silence still, of faint, far-off communication in a forgotten language. I strained to hear, to understand. . . .

All is rhythm, all is light. We can see by number, we can hear by LIGHT.

Now smoke the Pipe.

I did so, and after that sat empty, waiting, waiting, till before dawn the birds began to sing, meadow lark and others, and I knew the night had passed.

There followed a long hard hot day. Thirst became a problem, until I remembered I could draw on the water from streams I knew and loved, and also that my "family" would be drinking for me. Toward dusk Power Man and a helper came. They kneeled in silence outside the door, then Power Man came in and smudged me specially. He stuffed the Pipe, smudged it, smudged the lodge, went outside and sealed the flap with a longer ceremony. The second night of the second fast began.

The darkness was different this time, completely black, yet lighter in essence, not so claustrophobic. The walls of the shelter seemed to expand in a circle of lavender light, beyond which I could not see. Suddenly there was a great crashing at the flap and a thundering on the ground, like the entrance of Grandfather Buffalo to Ceremonies. The lavender light darkened to black, but the walls did not contract. The lodge was definitely larger, and there was a massive Being facing me.

I bowed my head and talked to It aloud, restating the reasons for which I was fasting to be a healing Pipe-Woman, also for Tsaviaya, his Sweat Lodge and his people. Then I waited, with all my essence, every cell and atom exposed to scrutiny.

When the blood replenished me again and I was able cautiously to relax the rigidity of awe, almost terror, I knew the test was passed or failed, the judgment, however it went, was over, the sentence, whatever it was, pronounced. Later I would learn what I should know. For the enduring moment all I could hold on to was the sincerity of my intent and the perfect justice of the Grandfathers.

This was only the second night of the second fast. More and deeper trials must lie ahead. Would I be able to pass through them?

"Deal only with the *Now*", a deep voice said. "Now is the time for you to smoke your Pipe."

This time it took the two matches, and for a moment the second match wavered. I asked the elementals of the fire to help me and the flame flared up, the tobacco caught with some unsteady puffing which slowly grew calm and regular. I smoked for the interdependence of created things, the willingness of nature spirits and other forces to come to our aid, and our obligation to reciprocate.

After the Pipe I sat in meditation. I was exhausted. I grew conscious of an overwhelming need for sustenance, for food, for drink, for sleep. "I am dehydrated," I whispered, "and down to the last atom of resistance."

"You can do it, you can do it," a chorus of small voices urged around me. It sounded like children, the Little Men of the Mountains. "No, I can't," I said. And then I heard my part-

Indian father from his place in the Spirit world, insisting "There's nothing like sticking it out to the end." And again, other voices, "We count on you. It's not just you. It's more important than you realize."

I called all the outposts of myself together, and grew centered, then I think I must have left in trance. The next I knew the door of the flap was open and Power Man was looking at me earnestly. I tried to smile, I tried to crawl forward, for a moment I couldn't manage it. Then I tried harder, reached the door and struggled upright to raise my arms to the sunrise.

Sunday June 13th

A very, very long day. The worst of it was broken by the Sweat which I could hear going on, with C.'s deep chanting. Presently Power Man, L. and C. came to the flap. Power Man entered and sat for a long time in silence, while the others kneeled outside. I knew that he was asking the Spirits whether I was being true and whether I would make it. Then he told me to inhale the smudge deeply. It was the same sweet grass, the "punk" they use for blessing food and blessing him when he lies beneath his turquoise blanket in the Ceremonies. I breathed it in as deeply as I could. He said his Arapaho prayer, then he fastened me in for the last long night.

It began to rain, a downpour on the shelter. The cold and the damp grew intense. But there was no total darkness this third night of the second fast. Black night outside, inside a sort of opalescence behind which the walls of the lodge receded indefinitely and the claustrophobia I shrank from with them.

I shut my eyes and counted twenty. When I opened them the light was still there, and now there seemed to be an amphitheatre, starting from the center, where in a sweat lodge the fire would be, and climbing in tiers to where I sat, for I sat high above the place where my body sat on the tule reeds. Now there were faces, miniature figures ranged below me, growing larger until they were life-sized in the high ring round me. I could not see them clearly, for they changed as I looked, now Indian, now white, now pulsating shadowy non-human faces, some smiling, mostly very grave.

At the bottom of the arena—it was like looking through the wrong end of a telescope—symbols were forming. First the Great Medicine Fire, then in the heart of the flames, the

Balance of the Four Great Directions. Then three circles form·
ed around the central fire ring. One was white, one was green
and one was yellow.

They faded. The amphitheater shrank and disappeared.
The pearly opalescent light changed to darkness. I was back
on the tule reeds, clutching my pipe. Now the cold and damp
struck in. I trembled. The walls of the small cramped fast
lodge shook and flapped with sudden gusts of rain and wind. I
groped for the two matches, lit the Pipe and prayed to the
Grandfathers for steadfastness, and understanding of the
things that I had seen. Then I sat numbly waiting for the
dawn.

Monday, 14th June

Came out triumphantly this morning and received a
wonderful message in the Sweat. "Go on as you're going, use
the Pipe as you've been using it, and things will come to you."
All my prayers in the fast were granted. I felt very weak, but
very full of joy.

20

Thursday, June 17th.

Three of the Canadians asked if they might fast, a two-night fast, and come out, when O. does. So we took them "in" to their fasting lodges, the same procession across the starlit fields, on the now familiar but always strange and magical journey under the stars, with meadowlark singing, to put them in, with the chanting and the prayers. We had to leap across a deep muddy ditch with rushing water, all in a decorous line, young and old.

It is always profoundly right and moving for me. Also right and moving was the Sweat for them, four rounds and no openings, during which each one spoke of the coming test and the reasons for which he was fasting: the choice of a new life, the rejection of evil, etc. The youngest's words were poignant. He said that he was a lonely man who didn't fit in well, and he was grateful for the friendly smiles he had received here. I thought "you and how many more, my brother!" But there we all were, gathered together from the ends of the earth for they, too, had travelled and lived on other continents, to sit here each in his place.

I was in the second row, in front, sitting sideways close to the flaming rocks, facing Power Man. I felt a new force and dignity surging through me, since the completion of my fast, and a new ability to bless.

Friday, June 18th.

Woke with the sun and smoked for the fasting ones. Then the simplicities of the little camp began. H. making Indian bread with strong skillful hands, in an iron pot over the open fire, flipping the dough about, talking all the while. Power Man's wife coming over to borrow change for the children to go to town. It's very hot. A week since I went into the fast.

Saturday, June 19th.

I woke before dawn and smoked my pipe and put the little stone man to worship. Then at sun-up I joined the others round our camp fire to wait for the four fasting men to be released. Soon they came across the fields and we all went into Sweat. It was a long, hot Sweat, with four pipes. I was exhausted, sitting in the front circle again, almost on the rocks.

We heard that the older man, the writer, was accepted by the Grandfathers to be trained as a Medicine Man, a healer, and would be told how to get himself ready to begin next year. He cried. The others were told they had done all right and would have their prayers answered.

After breakfast I rested in the camper. Power Man arrived with some mail for me. Not everyone has mail delivered by an Arapaho Medicine Man! I had this chance to talk to him, but as usual found I couldn't open up completely, though I wanted to. Years of stupid repressions, and besides I always feel he knows it all anyway, and a lot more behind that gentle smile.

Sunday, June 20th.

No Sweat today. Pow Wow tonight, to which we went. I was dubious about taking photographs, but was told by Power Man's wife that I should, for all of them. Now and then as I tried to take a particular man, with an extraordinary face, my flashbulb would fail for no reason except, as I supposed, he didn't choose to be taken. The same thing happened with Power Man's wife the day before. And sometimes in the past when I haven't wanted to be photographed, cameras have jammed, or films mysteriously been exposed to light, or rolls of them "lost." It's interesting, but I feel uncomfortable. I think this may have been a test and that I should have resisted or refused. (Later I learned that I was right, and none of them came out.)

Monday, June 21st.

Sweat this morning. Ceremonies tonight. Just one evening of it, during which those who were doctored and especially those who fasted, were "checked on." Asked, as I presented my flag, "What do you want, M?" I answered, "What I fasted for." and was told as I already heard in the Sweat, "your prayers, and what you vowed and fasted for are all granted."

At the ceremonies we were told again that all the fasts were good. We were thanked for fasting. We were told in detail about ourselves, and we were told the Californian group were taking a big blessing back with them.

In the middle of the day we had struck camp and packed. I would have liked to stay on a few days, but my Paiute family needed to get home. The camp disappeared without a trace, slowly, efficiently, and completely. The fire pit was covered in. The poles were carted off, the awnings folded and gone. No one could have told that anyone had ever paused here, let alone lived for two weeks with plenty of activity. I remembered being told once by a Micmac in Nova Scotia that a well-bred Indian passes through forests and through life without leaving a trace of himself behind. Here we were doing it, so that someone else today, or tomorrow or sometime, might camp here, as if on virgin land, and perhaps prepare as I did, to go into the fast.

Tuesday, June 22nd

Early this morning we pulled out, about five, and started on our long hot way. We crossed the salt flats in the heat of the day, as I dreaded, and finally reached higher and cooler ground.

I fasted twice more, once the next year, a two-night fast in California, on a reservation near Tsaviaya's, under the care of the man I had sat beside at my first fast. He was now a Medicine Man, with his own Sweat Lodge, which I attended regularly, and had since it was built. I will call him Eagle Man, because he was of the Eagle clan, going the Eagle Way. Unlike Tsaviaya who followed the Arapaho Way, of Grandfather Buffalo, Eagle Man followed the Paiute way of his native valley. I had attended his Sweat Lodge now for three years.

Many of the Indians who went to Tsaviaya's Sweat Lodge and the Ceremonies when Power Man came to lead them, also came to Eagle Man's Sweat, as well as others who came only to Eagle Man. The workings were different in a few respects, the Spirits who came in were different too, though Grandfather Buffalo and other Arapaho spirits also came, but more as visitors to the regional Powers.

Most of my Indian friends came to Eagle Man's Sweat, including the Paiute family who "stood behind me" for my three night fast. This time I was to make an extra two-night fast, for the Sweat Lodge and for a special misssion I would be making to the east.

Sunday, August 27th.

Sweat. I was committed to the Fast, and I told what I was fasting for. It was a strange waiting day, so far as weather goes, with an earthquake feeling, and there was a small one in the south. Eagle Man said I would be going up the mountain to fast beside the men. I found a perfect arrowhead, a small obsidian bird one.

Monday, August 28th

Walking today as usual in the field I saw a rainbow slowly growing until it was complete, stretching across the mountains, to the Sweat Lodge, and then to where I live. I took it for an omen. A gentle rain fell over me as I walked. Rain is a special blessing in this desert. The Indians say rain is a new beginning.

Thursday, August 31st.

Eagle Man has changed his mind. I am to fast, not on the mountain with the others, but because I am a woman, I will fast in the Sweat Lodge. I am disappointed.

Friday, 1st September.

It was decided, by Eagle Man, and announced in the Sweat that we would be taking this Lodge down and building a new one on new ground. I was fasting for this one to come into being and now I shall be spending the last night in it—strange. I told L. while we were eating that I was disappointed not to be out on the mountain, because I wanted to see the stars. She said "you will see plenty of stars in there."

During the Sweat we had, as usual, to say what we were fasting for. I said "For a blessing on the Sweat Lodge, and Eagle Man, and the people, and for a better harmony."

There is trouble being whipped up between Indians and whites. H. and R. have both succumbed to it, R. very badly. This made for a poor atmosphere for the start. But as soon as I was enclosed and began to "talk" to the Grandfathers, I knew that this fast was right and what I should be doing. There were many lovely things about it, that good gentle man, P., stuffing the Pipe for me, and helping to put me in, and all the friends who had come to bless me, and see me fastened up.

Because this was an extra fast, there was no Give-Away, physically, but in the two years since my first fast I had learned more about the real Give-Away. As Hyemeyohsts Storm points out in *Seven Arrows*: "All the things of the Universe Wheel have spirit and life, including the rivers, rocks, earth, sky, plants and animals. But it is only man, of all the Beings on the Wheel, who is a determiner. Our determining spirit can be made whole only through the learning of our harmony with all our brothers and sisters, and with all the other spirits of the universe. To do this we must learn to seek and to perceive. We must do this to find our place within the Medicine Wheel. To determine this place we must learn to Give-Away."

Later in the text there is this dialogue:

"You must find the People and offer them these gifts of understanding that you now see inside yourself," we hear the old man say.

"But what are these gifts?" we hear the little girl say.

"They are the understandings which you now perceive inside yourself, and which you must Give-Away to the People, so that they may also receive. Then they will no longer be starving for the Ways of Learning," the old man said.

With this in mind I entered the Sweat Lodge which was to be my fast lodge and Eagle Man sealed me in. He smudged me thoroughly with P.'s help, handed me the Pipe and went outside, fastening the flaps with the ritual flags and branches.

I settled myself on the tule reeds, centered and turned upward toward the Grandfathers, "talking" of the reasons for the fast, to heal the new disharmony which was more important than my mission to the east. After I finished "talking" I chanted. Then I sat still, waiting,. The wind rose suddenly. It blew so hard that I thought a gale of hurricane force must be sweeping in. The sides of the shelter bellied in and out. The willows holding up the covering strained and shrieked. The noise was ferociously alive. Now it was a black, frightening night in there, lonely, rough and tough.

I sat as far as I could from the cannonading walls, gripping the Pipe, asking for the Grandfathers to protect me, praying for the fast and courage to complete it rightly. There would be no difficulty about staying awake! The point was to survive in the fragile shelter from what might be a tornado. I told myself that I was not afraid—apprehensive now and then, but not afraid—but if this had been my first experience of the fast I might have been terrified. I might have tried to break out and run for cover. I wondered if that was what Eagle Man expected me to do. I thought of the others on the mountainside in more flimsy shelters than mine and wondered how they fared. We all expected to be tested, but not by this-plane danger, not by hurricane.

I was disconcerted that there were no lights or other manifestations from the Grandfathers. I felt chagrined that the Spirits did not come in. I tried to think that They couldn't come because of the hurricane, but that was nonsense. I wondered if They disapproved of me and had abandoned me as Eagle Man and P. and all the others seemed to have done. Surely no one could be sleeping through this tremendous storm. Why didn't someone come to check on me? But no one did, and after awhile the wind abated and there was only heavy sweeping rain.

Dawn came at last, and Eagle Man to set me free. I half expected some inquiry about the night, but no one broke the ritual silence, and when I stepped outside to greet the Sun there was no trace of any damage. Even the ground had dried from the heavy rain.

Later I learned that the night had been exceptionally calm and quiet, not a breath stirred in the valley or on the mountain. Nor was there any rain.

Saturday, Sept. 2nd.

After a long, hot, desolate, uncomfortable day, I came to the evening weary and rather dreading another night of violence and total blackout, but when I was closed in I found that there was a light, a sort of soft dimness with side flashes of brilliance. I was relieved and grateful.

After I had prayed, a voice said "you may lie down on the tules if you do not sleep." I put the Pipe in the hollow of my arm and lay down on my back. Suddenly the top of the Sweat Lodge went away and I could see a whole sky full of moving lights, stars and flashing lines and swirls.

I lay conscious of where I was, with my eyes open. When I shut them the sight went away as it normally does. When I opened them, there the whole sky was again.   I looked to left or right, that part of the lodge went away and I saw the moving lights and stars. It was a lovely and kind sort of sky. The stars were more beautiful than our stars, because they were in motion. They seemed to be dancing. I thought, too, that they were laughing.

It lasted a long time, while I lay contentedly watching and being grateful to see this new part of the universe the planet must be sailing through, unless these were our stars, in another, lighter dimension. Then the roof closed down again, opening spasmodically to show me wierd landscapes, none of which I could see long enough to understand or to recognize. Then there were faces. When these became frightening I gripped the Pipe and started to pray hard, and they went away.

I spent the rest of the night aware and awake and not tired but very happy.

Sunday, Sept. 3rd.

The long night came to an end. I was freed and stepped out to face the moon and stars, in a fresh black night. A little later came the Sweat, in what had been my fast lodge. We all had to make our reports. After the two men had spoken I tried to describe my experience and there was a great stir among the circle. L. saw an opening above my head. I saw another strange thing, the floor of the Sweat Lodge was suddenly shell-like and slanting upward like an arena, and the fire shrank to a much smaller compass. I wonder if I am developing new sight, and will it come only at sweats and fasts or other times?

After the Sweat, the hostile ones talked of a parade and other worldly things, but R. and some others were genuinely pleased for me, R. said "Now it opened up for you. It didn't take long. (eight years!). Now you are really Indian" L. said "Didn't I tell you you would see plenty stars?" Others congratulated me.

I ate and drank. Weary but not overcome I drove home.

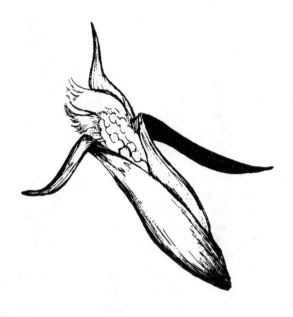

21

About two weeks before my four-night fast, I went to see Eagle Man with a problem. Off and on over a long period I had been going through a strange experience. It began upon the mountain when I was smoking the Pipe. A sudden blow on my left shoulder almost knocked me over, as though a great bird had plummeted down upon me. I opened my eyes, startled, but there was nothing to be seen, though I could feel the grip of talons and the weight of whatever it was still there.

I was startled, but I realized how often there were inexplicable, to the 'logical mind', phenomena when smoking. I closed my eyes and finished the Pipe, during which the something heavy sat still on my shoulder, gripping it firmly. I expected it to go away when the Pipe was over, but It didn't. It sat on my shoulder all the way down the mountain. When I reached the bottom It lifted.

Now and then It came again, always to the left shoulder, not only when I was on the mountain, smoking. Once it came when I was in a group of people, who noticed nothing strange, though I felt my manner must reveal distraction. It was only when it was constantly with me that I felt I must get advice. It is hard, with our false training and brain-washing, not to suspect self-hallucination or even mental illness, when things like this happen. So I went to Eagle Man.

"I seem," I said hesitantly, "to be conscious of a bird on my left shoulder, or behind it."

He looked at me quizzically, as though to say, as he sometimes did, "well? So what?"

After a silence I went on, "Is there something I should do?"

"You could feed It," he said, "It gets hungry, same as us."

This was a new idea to me.

I asked "With what?"

He said eagles didn't like tobacco as "the others" do. He said "corn wheat, pi-nuts, sometimes fish."

    didn't matter who ate the actual offering, bird or little animal, the essence would go to the right Eagle.

We talked of what I would be fasting for. I found it hard to put into words—to be a healer-helper, a consoler of miseries, a woman medicine doctor, in other words "more of the same", to go on taking care of those who were in my Pipe.

He said "Go on as you are going. It's up to you. No one can tell you what to do."

I said, "Thank you for all you have taught me."

He said, "Don't thank me. Thank the Grandfathers."

I said "All the same I thank you, and the Grandfathers." He said that I should have two Pipes, one I would use only by myself, and another for smoking with others.

My diary says: *November 16th*

Snowing on the mountains. At noon I said I was going to smoke and I had a wonderful Pipe, alone, which I did need. I put an ear of corn into a tree and as I left the special place a crow came and swooped down to where I had been, while another circled overhead. Then both came and glided round and round over my head, and over T. and D. who were walking a little in front. Finally, after a lovely exhibition, they moved off northward. I gather that the corn was acceptable. Perhaps it is a crow I have, a "little black eagle", but I have the impression of gray and brown, and bigger than a crow.

November 18th.

Sun out by fits and starts, but weather not settled yet. It rained and blustered all night. This is the date that I received the special ring of the two-headed eagle, long years ago. Since then I have become a travelling journeyman, a Pipe-woman, wandering out on missions. "How strange it seems, and new."

November 21st.

I took the Pipe up the hill to the favorite place beside the rushing stream. I put out corn and sardines. No bird visibly came, but there was a great attentive peace during the smoking and the talons on my shoulder.

November 23rd.

There was a crow here early in the morning. I put out corn. Later in the day I went up to the favorite place, but smoked in a different, more open area. I put out sardines and corn. There was an eagle circling as I arrived. I asked for help and guidance about the coming fast, that I might come to it properly prepared.

Sunday, November 25th.

The Sweat today was a little inharmonious for me because of things H. and P. said, or intimated, about Eagle Man, and the general ugly feeling there seemed to be against "non-Indians", who, H. said, can never be anything more than occasional visitors. This is sad for the group of young white people who have been coming for several years, and for me after thirteen years of friendship. We must try to remember that all things prepare us for the next stage of lighter, better vibrations.

November 27th.

I went to Eagle Man to talk about the coming fast. It was a strong and joyful Pipe tonight. I put out corn for the Winged One who goes with the Pipe. Eagle Man said today that he might call on me now for help. I said, inadequately, "at *any* time."

I realize that this four-night fast is the culminating one, the last that I am obligated to make.

November 28th.

Drove with D. to a good place for smoking, and afterwards to eat. D. said "Look at that little critter—squirrel or something—on that rock." I said "It can't be a squirrel, the distance is too far and the trees at the base of the rock too high. Perhaps it's an enormous owl. It has those ears."

We got the glasses from the car and it was a mountain lion. He sat majestic on the rock, surveying us, turning his head from side to side. We were evidently eating in his dining room, for there were bones of little animals all about, and D. found a tuft of his hair under a tree. She took it to be identified later. He was a magic sight, so near the road, so free and wild.

Later, in the moonlight, coming down the pass we saw a deer.

"All coming to your fast," D. said.

We talked about fasting. D. has not yet fasted. We agreed that it was a joyful experience and not at all a deprivation: that it was one way of expanding consciousness and getting in touch with "Those Above." D., being white, is troubled that the Sweat Lodge may be closed to her, after three years of steady attendance.

November 30th, 1973

My fast day opened gray and veiled and snowy, but cleared into sun on the snow-wrapped mountains, blue sky and small white clouds going northward. Crows went northward too, small birds feasted on the birdseed in the garden.

Little Black Eagle has just come through the garden checking after me. This place is so beautiful! I give thanks for it every day and will give more tonight.

Went up to the reservation around five, and then to the Sweat, a good one, a hot one, with no openings. Then the meal, and after it, around nine-thirty, Eagle Man "put me in." A great storm came up, purely physical this time, all night rain slashed against the north wall, though the wind was from the south. I had my fasting blanket close around me but still I was cold.

Two fiery Wheels appeared, one over where Eagle Man sits

at Sweat, and one where P. sits opposite him. They were flashing, and on the rims were lights like sparklers. One went round the lodge, then they disappeared. They were the only vision this night, but it was never totally dark. There was the lavender-gray light.

I meditated upon Wheels, the Great Medicine Wheel, the Zodiac, life in the sacred round. Then I smoked the Pipe, and a comforting warmth spread through my body. I had always been too hot in the fasts before. The ordeal of cold is harder.

In the morning Eagle Man came to take me out. I stood and prayed toward the sun. Then I lay dozing through the long, long, cold day. In the afternoon a flock of small blackbirds walked by, going round and round the altar, they peeked in, chattering. Then they disappeared, and suddenly an enormous magpie, fat and lustrous, trotted by. They had to go through a lot of maneuvering to get where I could see them through the small opening. So also later I caught a glimpse of Eagle Man pointing upward, and put my face to the door to see. There was the Small Eagle circling over the fast lodge.

Night came at last, and Eagle Man "put me in" again, this time with more ceremony, and P. to assist. I was smudged with the sweet grass "punk", weaving all around, past my face, and up and down my blanket, over my Pipe, then total blackness and cold, so very cold this night.

The visions, when they came, were small luminous clouds floating round the lodge and faces, of many kinds, mostly Indian, but some white, and pain and cold and prayers, and periods of trance-like "travelling" from which I brought back confused impressions of the burning, turning Wheels and H's face. (I heard later that he had died very suddenly at the time that I was seeing him.) When faces come it is to receive a blessing or to give a message, so I blessed him.

This day too was long and cold, and I was hungry, but even more thirsty for something hot to drink. Meditation was difficult. "Abstinence is detachment from the body and senses, say the Sages but it is hard to be detached on the third day of an Indian fast.

Night came at last, and with it Eagle Man and P. to "put me in." Through the opening I could see the sky behind them.

There was a great cradle, circling round the moon, with some geometrical lines through it, a very strange effect.

Then the long night began. I wasn't cold this time, the wind had dropped. My fast blanket grew wonderfully warm and comforting. The lodge was dark, no lavender light, nothing but solitude, endurance, and a few faint flashes. I braced myself for testing, but there was nothing difficult. It was a quiet night, except for coyotes howling near and one or two blows against the walls.

Somehow the blackness and the quietude were more significant, more penetrating to the inner being than anything undergone before. I felt that I was travelling, travelling, travelling, through Cosmic space.

Toward dawn, so far as I could tell, from a rooster crowing, I smoked the Pipe. Eagle Man came to take me out. I was weak as I stood to greet the sun, and through the long, long day, I dozed and made resolutions to do better through the coming night. One must not be passive in the fast. It is an opportunity to stretch the consciousness which may not come again.

Eagle Man came to talk to me in the afternoon, and brought a little figure he was making, a small elephant, stocky, charming, about an inch long. I must remember to tell him that there were elephants here in the valley in prehistoric times, if he doesn't know that. Not many people do.

Then darkness came again, and he put me in, with the burning sweet grass and all the careful blessing and said goodnight and fastened the door. Behind it I sat up, centering myself for this last night of the fast, which began in total darkness. I prayed for what I was fasting for and for everything else I could remember, and for the names and faces flashing to me.

Presently there was one wheel and lines of light, and again the lavender light took away the darkness. I knew that the night outside had a bright moon on the snowy mountains, but when the top of the lodge went away the night was black and the stars dim, not like last year's bright ones. They were moving gravely in a more stately dance. I lay down, to see them better, but I began to doze, and so sat up, holding my pipe, with the stem upward, and prayed aloud, hard.

Then the top slowly closed and the lodge returned to total darkness. Suddenly I felt that I was gathered into the force-field of the world, of Mother Earth.

"The world is but a single day in which we are fasting", came to me. I felt that I had been surveyed by the Grandfathers and come into the presence of the Lords of Karma, that I had been judged, although I would not know the judgment yet. I gave thanks for the Grandfathers, their help and their protection and the glimpses that they give us of themselves, to remind us of Wakan-Tanka. I gave thanks for the Lords of Karma, their wisdom, their justice and their love for us. I asked forgiveness for the shortcomings of the fast.

Then Eagle Man was at the opening. It was still dark when he took me out, with pre-dawn light on the horizon. He went to light the fire for the sweat. I came back and went in again to smoke the Pipe. My lips and throat were dry, and I was weak, but the Pipe was comforting and strong, stronger than I had ever known it be. Presently Eagle Man told me to go and change for Sweat. I staggered to my cold camper. He followed, bringing a bucket of hot stones to warm it up for me, thoughtful, concerned man. He asked me about the night. I told him. He said I must repeat it in the lodge.

People began to arrive. I changed into clean sweat clothes, and went to stand outside the door, by the fire.

Before the Sweat began, Eagle Man reported that as far as he could tell, everything had gone well. The spirits had come to his house and called him by name. Then he asked for my report, and I gave it as well as I could, through parched mouth.

H. sitting beside me went into a long Paiute prayer with many "Eveleenies" sprinkled in it. I wish I knew what she was saying! She went into English about the Wheels. "Whirlies are not from *our* Mother," she said firmly, "Whirlies come from some other Grandfather for Eveleenie." There was a chorus of Hy-ehs, and more comments in Paiute.

I went through Sweat well, though I felt weak and faint. Later, when I had eaten a little and rested, a surge of strength came back, and I knew that my Pipe was more powerful. I drove home feeling spent but deeply satisfied.

22

After I had seen the "whirlies" in the fast, I was interested when Eagle Man told me to go to the Coso Range, where there were many petroglyphs, to smoke the Pipe and make offerings to the Grandfathers there.

It was a difficult assignment, for this territory is within the Naval Weapons Center at China Lake and it is only possible to visit it in short guided tours of groups of people. I applied for one of these, with a friend to help me. Our cover-up was that she was to write an article on petroglyphs, and I was to take the photographs.

I packed the Pipe, my Medicine Bag, paraphernalia and offerings in an outsize shoulder holdall. There was no room for anything else, but I stuck a camera in my pocket, in case. After our permits were checked, we were herded into the canyon by two guides. At first it seemed as though it might be impossible to do more than walk through it, with the Pipe giving its secret blessing on what we happened to pass, but presently the tour began to split up into smaller groups, the guides going ahead with eager beavers, the stragglers dropping behind. We managed to come last, pausing now and then to take pictures and notes of rocks with striking glyphs. But there seemed no chance to do what I was sent for, without exposing the Pipe to indiscriminate curiosity.

Suddenly a crow flew over the canyon's rim, swooped low, cawed urgently and darted up a side opening we had not seen. We waited until all the backs were turned, then slipped aside to follow him. It was a narrow, winding space between huge rocks, empty of petroglyphs until we turned a corner, and there, spread on three sides of an open space were Medicine Men, horned sheep, ladders, and three dominating "whirlies", forming a triangle.

My friend didn't need to say, "Quick, quick! This is the place!" I was already sitting down crosslegged facing the triangle, tugging at my shoulderpack. I got out the shell used to burn sage, the Pipe in its bag, tobacco, and the offerings of corn, and other things.

"If you'll sit there," I said, "you'll block the view and be able to warn me."

At that moment the crow reappeared, and lit on a rock above us. "I'll warn you," it seemed to say.

I lit the sage, smudged us and everything to be used, ceremonially filled the Pipe and began to smoke. I asked the Grandfathers of that ancient place to smoke with me if they would, I said I brought blessing and offerings from a present-day Medicine Man who would have come there, if he could, to build a sweat lodge and conduct the old rites among the old symbols. I asked that the smoke of the Pipe might go far and wide through the canyon, protecting the petroglyphs from pollution and vandalism; that it might so permeate these rocks and these paths that all who wandered near might feel the presence of the Grandfathers and turn themselves toward Wakan-Tanka.

I felt very strong presences round me and as usual lost all sense of time and place. The smoke spiralled upward among the rocks. It was a wonder it didn't bring everybody running.

Fires of any kind were strictly forbidden especially during this time of drought. It was what my friend dreaded as she sat anxiously shielding me. But I have found the Pipe is always protected when it is necessary to smoke it. I "talked" in peace to the Great Ones, and knew that They heard.

As I sat, still dazed from the far journey I had taken into timeless time, the crow cawed urgently, flapped its wings and flew away. I thrust the Pipe out of sight beneath the pack, took the offerings and scrambled up the rocks toward where the crow had been. Half way up I found a flat surfaced stone, with a hollow in it. Here I placed the corn, the tobacco, and the rest, turning in the ritual way to the four corners before the tramp of feet, very near, but no one appeared until everything was hidden. Then what they saw was a photographer engaged in taking pictures of horned sheep.

"There are better ones further on," someone said.

"Did you get what you wanted?" the tour guide asked as he shepherded us out and saw us safely to the carpark.

I said "yes," but I would have liked to come back alone or with Eagle Man, and do the whole canyon thoroughly, and spend the night there, with a sunrise Sweat the next day, as it must have been in olden times. We did get into another part of the range, at another time with a small group of Indians and whites, and Eagle Man did hold a Sweat Lodge there, of a limited kind, but not among the petroglyphs.

But the Indians can't use the hot springs there, which are fast drying up because they can't.

23

Some weeks later, I went to see Eagle Man, taking him my albums with the photographs of petroglyphs, pictographs and the Rock Drawings of Nevada, for him to see the "whirlies." He was interested and drove his wife and me to see the ones he had found on Sunday, in his territory.

Sure enough they were the whirlies I had seen in the fast. We talked together of their meanings and applications to our work which was increasing for both of us. More and more people came to his Sweat Lodge. More and more people were asking me for help. I had a telephone put into my hut and it was a rare day that it did not ring several times.

"My son is ill. Will you put him into your Pipe?" "I have lost my job. Will you put it into your Pipe?" "May I come and see you? I am in trouble." "A terrible thing has happened. I need help." "Will you come and bless my house? There is a bad feeling in it." "My mother is dying." "My daughter has died." 'Please help my son, he is taking drugs."

On one exceptional day an emergency call came from Eagle Man for a special doctoring Sweat. He had injured his back. He asked me to bring my Pipe. When we entered the Sweat Lodge he told me to sit next to him, and then to give him my Pipe. He explained to the people present that this Pipe has a special power attached to it, that if we used it in a certain way an Eagle would come in. He handed it back to me, and I did what I was supposed to do.

Then he asked me to doctor him with the Feather, his great Eagle Feather. I beat upon his back, until he told me it was enough, it was good. While I was "doctoring" him, the people were singing, and P. was pouring water on the rocks, so that the Sweat proceeded through the four rounds.

Once I felt the talons on my shoulder, and several times I heard the beat of wings about the Lodge. So did others, and now it was an open secret that this Pipe has an Eagle going with it, a small one, what non-Indians call a red-tailed hawk. When we came out of Sweat one was circling above the area.

Next day Eagle Man's back was better. He was able to go to work. I went up the mountain with my Pipe. A friend joined me. It was dusk but still light enough to see a magnificent coyote, completely unafraid of us. In fact when we drew nearer to him he sat down to get a better look. Up the hill, though it was cold everywhere else, it was warm and comfortable by the stream. After a good and happy Pipe, I left corn and sardines for the Eagle.

Sunday, December 23rd.

To Sweat. The only woman among a crowd of men. H. was there and Eagle Man's nephew from the south. It was a good Sweat. L. was away in Nevada among her people, the same hostiles who are stirring her and so many up against "non-Indians." P. said in the Sweat that a small, pretty Eagle had been seen around the Lodge last Sunday. He didn't say why it came, but the emphasis he put on it may have been informative to those who hadn't been there. He described it flying round inside. Then he smiled at me.

Sunday, December 30th.

To Sweat and a wonderful one it was. But afterwards Eagle Man's nephew came to talk to me in my car. He is the Indian

version of "angry young man", going to a college where he
learns only the bad things the whites have done. He told me
that all non-Indians should leave the Sweat, that Eagle Man's
Lodge would die if whites continued to go there. I said what I
could, that Eagle Man was helping and healing *all* who came
there, regardless of their skins, that his own people had not
always stood behind him, an understatement even he recognized. He said "The whites only come out of curiosity." I said,
"Not these young people." I added that without them and their
steady help and attendance the Sweat Lodge would have
been weakened. I said that I understood how he felt, but did
he remember the happy days before all this whipped-up
hatred was brought in from outside?

He did. He had mixed emotions. He began to cry. I said if
Eagle Man wanted non-Indians not to come to his Sweat
Lodge, and told us so, we would stay away. He said he didn't
think of me as a non-Indian. I said I counted myself a human
being, neither Indian nor non-Indian, and thought of him and
everyone as *people*. I said that Eagle Man's vow at the time of
his fast had been for a Sweat Lodge for *all* regardless of skins,
and that I too had fasted for this Sweat Lodge. I said non-
Indians had given wood and labor and loving respect.

After a silence we smiled at one another, wistfully, and he
got out of the car. But how sad! I know these Indians are
expecting the Great Grandfather to come, the end of the
world, when all the whites will be swept away, except a few,
"liberated whites", token, second-class citizens.

I thought of Wovoka's vision, who first spoke to them about
the coming new world. The essence of his teaching, as he
gave it to the world, was that "the time will come when the
whole Indian race, living and dead, will be reunited upon a
regenerated earth, to live a life of happiness, forever free from
death, disease and misery. The white race will have no part in
this, and will be left behind with the other things of earth that
have served their temporary purpose, or else will cease en-
tirely to exist. Meanwhile the people must dance the sacred
dance, must do no harm to anyone, do right always, work well
with the whites and get along with them until the Day arrives.
All things will be taken care of by the Great Spirit. Above all

you must not fight, there must be no war." James Mooney
heard this directly from Wovoka in 1892.

Porcupine, the Cheyenne Medicine Man who visited
Wovoka and received the teachings directly from him, reports
Wovoka as saying:

> "My father told me the earth was getting old and worn
> out and the people getting bad and that I was sent to
> renew everything as it used to be and make it better.
> He also told us that our dead were to be resurrected;
> that they would all come back to the earth and that the
> earth would be made big enough to contain us all; that
> we must tell all the people we met about these things.
> He spoke to us about fighting, and said that was bad
> and we must keep from it; that the earth was to be all
> good hereafter, and we must all be friends with one
> another. He told us that we were not to quarrel or fight
> or strike each other or shoot one another; that the
> whites and Indians were to be all one people."

Some thought Wovoka meant until the great Day of the
Separation arrived. Others, including several Medicine Men
of different tribes believed that the good and great and humble of any race would be saved, that in fact "the meek—(the
gentle)—will inherit the earth."

Wovoka and the other Holy Men and Women seemed to be
forecasting the coming of the new earth and the new heaven,
or as others put it, nowadays, the entry of the planet and all
upon it into the Aquarian Age.

In 1892, involved as they were in the aftermaths of a bitter
defeat, savage treatment, broken treaties, unkept promises
and general shameful behavior of the conquering whites, it
would have been hard for most Indians to conceive of the
whites they encountered entering the new earth, yet many,
then as now, were aware that the new earth and the new
heaven would not be apportioned on the basis of pigmentation, nor confined to any racial, national or religious
group. This is the mistake made through the ages, that the
truth belongs to one segment of humanity alone.

As they began to encounter this problem of rejection and
hostility toward them as non-Indians, judged solely by their

skins, I was saddened for the young whites who had found the
Sweat Lodge over the years, and who were living the life of the
Medicine Wheel, while many of those agitating to exclude
them did not give Eagle Man steady support, nor ask for a
Pipe, nor fast, nor come to the Sweats. I began rereading the
teachings and words of the Great Medicine Men like Black
Elk, and Rolling Thunder, who at about this time spoke to an
audience of nearly three thousand men, with a message of
brotherhood, "the beginning of a oneness, a true spiritual
sharing between the Indian and the non-Indian."

"We are keepers of the land," Rolling Thunder said. "We say
there is room for everyone, that we are supposed to live as
brothers and share. That is the way it should be. We are
supposed to work together to make life good for all of us, all
who live upon this Mother Earth."

He went on to say that there was much the white race must
do "to change some of the stupid laws that have repressed my
people . . . and help put things back in their proper order"
before some of the knowledge of spiritual things could be
revealed. Then he added:

"I started moving among many different people of many
different races. I have met some people who are on a very high
spiritual plane like some of our medicine people. There are
certain signs and indications when one meets the right ones,
and sometimes it isn't even necessary to talk. Race and language makes no difference; the barriers are gone when persons can come together on high spiritual levels."

This talk is reported in Doug Boyd's book, *Rolling Thunder*.

Since my Indian friends were mostly Paiutes, they inherited
their tradition of the coming Change to the world from their
great Holy Man, Wovoka, born sometime between 1856 and
1858, in Mason Valley, Nevada. He never left his native region. Those who wished to hear his teachings had to go to
him.

His knowledge came to him in vision trances of which he
had many. The most important of these long cataleptic-seem-
ing seizures coincided with a total eclipse of the sun, on
January 1st, 1889. The Paiutes were awed and frightened by
this "death of the sun". The going away of their prophet at

such a time impressed them greatly and added to his growing authority.

He lay for four days and four nights seemingly dead. When he returned to consciousness on the morning of the fifth day, he told his wife and those who had watched by his body, that he had seen the Great Holy, and all the people who were dead, in another world; that Numin'a had told him to go back to his people and teach them a new dance, that if they danced it well and faithfully they would be able to go to the other world as he did and see their dead ones, too.

"This dance that we teach you," the Grandfathers told him, "has never been danced before. It is the Spirit Dance of the Other World."

The people must dance it for four nights and the morning of the fifth day. It must be danced in a circle facing inwards, with men and women dancers, hand in hand, first a man, then a woman, then a man. The faces of the dancers must be painted with sacred paint from the ochre-colored rocks. This is the same "paint" still taken from Coso and other places for healing and ceremonial purposes. I was given a supply of it when I received my healing stone. It is a basic part of the Medicine Bag.

There are also in the Coso region petroglyphs and incised rocks showing dancing figures, hand in hand, using the same step that is in use today. These petroglyphs are estimated by archeologists and other "authorities" who have studied the area to be at least 5000 years old. But many believe them to be much older, showing that Wovoka was reviving among his people a traditional dance of ancient times, which is also universal.

He recognized this. He said his teachings were "alla same Jesus", and that he would dance in the circle with his people as Jesus danced with his disciples. There was no way, in 1889, that Wovoka could have come by the knowledge beginning to be revealed to us, and even now not widely known, that Jesus danced a special dance in a circle with his disciples, a Cosmic Dance, a Dance of the Spirit World. This could only have come to Wovoka through the source of all his knowledge, his vision-trances.

There were songs to go with the dancing, sacred songs which he would teach his people, and they must sing them when they danced. Paiute singing is slow and stately, like the circling of an eagle. There is a plaintive depth in it that well suits the slow and solemn step of the Ghost Dance, as whites have named it. The dancers move from right to left, clockwise, sunwise, lifting the left foot hardly off the ground, moving it slightly to the left, bringing the right foot exactly into the place which the left foot has just abandoned. The Shoshoni call it the "dragging dance".

The purpose of it was to send as many people as possible into a deep trance, so that they could visit their dead relatives and friends, and bring back confirmation of Wovoka's teachings about the land of the spirits. Also, and this was the vital point, by faithfully dancing they would help bring about "the coming of a new world."

James Mooney observed:

"the manner of the final change and the distruction of the whites has been variously interpreted as the doctrine was carried from its original center. East of the mountains it is commonly held that a deep sleep will come on the believers, during which the great catastrophe will be accomplished, and the faithful will awake on a new earth. The Shoshoni of Wyoming say this sleep will continue four days and nights and that on the morning of the fifth day all people will open their eyes in a new world where both races will dwell together forever. The Cheyenne, Arapaho, Kiowa, and others say that the new earth with all the resurrected dead from the beginning, and with the buffalo and elk, and other game upon it, will come from the west and slide over the surface of the present earth, as the right hand might slide over the left. As it approaches, the Indians will be carried upward and alight on it by the aid of the sacred dance feathers which they wear in their hair and which will act as wings to bear them up. They will then become unconscious for four days, and on waking will find themselves with their former friends in the midst of all the old time surroundings."

Sitting Bull, the Arapaho Medicine Man, thought that this new Earth as it advances will be preceded by a wall of fire which will drive the whites across the water to their original and proper countries, while the Indians will be enabled by means of the sacred feathers to surmount the flames and reach the regenerated land. The fire will be extinguished by a rain continuing for twelve days.

The numbers connected with the teachings, are interesting, the fours and the twelves, also the shapes, the circles. It seems to me that the "sacred feathers" by which the Indians will be carried upward may also refer to the aura, the halo, the helmet of salvation which would reveal others entitled to surmount the flames, and be easily recognizable, by Those in charge of the operation.

None of my Indian friends have ever discussed the Ghost Dance with me, perhaps because of its implications of total destruction for the white race to which I legally belong. None of them admit to any knowledge of such a dance, or even of the prophet Wovoka. But we are not deceived by this tactful omission. They know that I know much about Wovoka, and the coming of the new age.

The dance which placed so many of his people into direct contact with the Spirit World, continued in secret through the days of the persecution, when he was being hunted by white soldiers with orders to kill him and put an end to his "war dance."

I also know that it is still danced today, more and more widely, with more and more fervor, all over Turtle Island.

There are many accounts of the Ghost Dances on different occasions, and some of the songs have come down to us, as for example, the song composed by Pa-guadal, "Red Buffalo", at a Dance held on Walnut Creek in the summer of 1893, under the direction of the prophet Pa-ingya. This is a Kiowa song.

I scream because I am a bird,
I scream because I am a bird,
I bellow like a buffalo,
I bellow like a buffalo,
The boy will rise up,
The boy will rise up.

The purpose of the dance was to gain contact with Red
Buffalo's son who had recently died. Red Buffalo was a
member of the Eagle Dance and followed the Eagle way—"I
scream because I am a bird," but his father was a Buffalo
Medicine Man, who had left his power to his son. Therefore
Red Buffalo, although he was an Eagle, could and did "bellow
like a buffalo."

The white man reporting this incident thought that the Indians were expecting an actual physical appearance of the
dead boy, and he remarks, "but the boy was not resurrected."
But of course the meeting between the father and the son took
place in the Spirit World, after Red Buffalo went into trance.

There is a song brought back by a Caddo girl who visited the
Spirit land and saw all her dead friends there. When she had
to leave, to rejoin her physical body, lying on the ground in
trance, her spirit-friends wept.

And another Caddo Ghost Dance song:-
Come on Caddo we are all going up
Come on Caddo we are all going up
To the great village, He'e'ye!
To the great village, He'e'ye!
With our Father above.
With our Father above
Where he dwells on high, He'e'ye!
Where our Mother dwells, He'e'ye!

It was sung near the beginning or the early middle of the
Caddo Ghost Dance to remind the people of the purpose of the
dance. The 'great village above' is the spirit land, a great
encampment, the Celestial City, Jerusalem the Golden. Our
Mother is the Earth, who also has her place in heaven.

The road to this Spirit World is the Milky Way, over which
the souls of the dead travel. A Kiowa Ghost song starts:
My Father shows me the road,
My Father shows me the road . . .

Whenever "the road" is mentioned in these songs it refers to
the transition after death. For some tribes this road which the
soul must travel to rejoin the relatives and friends in the Spirit
land, is a rainbow Bridge from this world to the next, similar to
the medieval "Brig o' Dread", between the earth and Purga-

tory. The dances referred to in many of the songs mean the
dances of the dead with their relatives and friends, a similar
concept to the Dancing of the Blessed in Fra Angelico's painting, the reunion of souls with their guardian angels, of the
Indian dead and their guardian Grandfathers.

Wovoka remained in hiding, moving from place to place,
eventually emerging cautiously to live near Walker Lake,
away from settlements, in a place where it would be possible
for remnants of his people and those who could escape from
surveillance on their reservations to join in dancing the sacred Dance of the Spirit World, from which he now excluded
all whites.

He began to occupy himself with the burial customs of the
Paiutes which, like the burial rites common to other tribes, he
condemned as cruel and unpleasing to the Grandfathers.

"When your friends die, you must not kill your horses,
must not gash your bodies with knives, nor let your
wives cut off their hair and be made to bleed. When
your friends die, you must not weep, because you will
all be united again."

Sarah Winnemucca describes her grandfather's death thus:

"At midnight, which was told by the seven stars reaching the same place that the sun reaches at midday, he
turned and twisted without opening his eyes. The doctor* said "He has spoken his last words, he has given
his last look, his spirit is gone: watch his lips, he will
speak as he enters the Spirit-land." And so he did, or
at least he seemed to. His lips moved as if he was
whispering. I wish to say that it is the belief of my
people that the spirit speaks as it goes on. They say if
a child has a mother or a father in the Spirit-land he
will cry as his soul enters.

"Now came the burial. Everything he had was put into the
grave with him. His body was put into blankets when it was
ready to be put into the grave, and after he was buried six of
his horses were killed."

All the possessions of the dead were burned, and usually
the house in which he died was burned so many families put
their dying outside, in specially built shelters, in order not to
have to burn down the home. Some changed the doors and

windows, as a symbolical destruction of the old and rebuild-
ing of the new.

Instead of these old customs Wovoka decreed that there
would be the Cry Dance as the Paiutes practice it today.

I shall never dance the Eagle Dance in this life, though I
have watched it danced, nor the Sun Dance, though I have
seen dancers preparing for it, but I have danced the Cry
Dance, several times, and these experiences have revealed to
me what it must be like for the participants of the great ceremonial dances, especially the Sun Dance.

24

The Cry-Dance is danced in a circle, but differs from the Spirit Dance of the Other World, in that no one touches another; the dancers follow each others' backs, and they move counter sunwise.

I went to my first Cry Dance in 1964, at the beginning of my association with the Paiutes. I knew that it was a funeral service for a much respected man, and that it would be acceptable for me to attend if I came with the Presbyterian Minister to one of the reservation missions who was to conduct the Christian service the day after the Cry Dance.

So on a cold and windy November night beneath a climbing moon, I stood in a group of onlookers, on a slope overlooking a cleared space with a big fire burning in the center of it. On one side there was a typical government-built box house where the family lived, beyond that the outhouse, and some indistinct sheds with shapes of cars and tractors round them.

The minister and his daughter went into the house to greet the bereaved family. Afterward I saw them both enter the circle standing round the fire, near a row of men in blankets and overcoats. These were the Cry-Dance Singers.

Presently the singing began, the dancers in the circle moved forward slowly, one behind the other, their left sides to the fire, holding something in their hands. Now and then they raised it above their heads, now and then they lowered it to their knees, in response to changes in the singing, but mostly they held it in front of them, fingers upward, elbows to their sides. It was too dark to see exactly what it was, even in the glow from the fire, but it seemed to be different colored strips of cloth.

The chief singer shouted "Heu!" and the singing and the dancing ceased. The dancers turned toward the fire to warm themselves. A few slipped aside and went into the house. Others took their places. The Chief Singer said "He ya!" Everything resumed. The song was different but the dance step seemed to be the same stately step forward, half step back, balance and on. It reminded me a little of the Chinese T'ai Chi Chih, especially the step that goes with the Six Healing Sounds. I began to think of the similarities between ancient peoples in their rhythmic approach to life.

There was another pause. A group came out of the house, two men supporting a woman between them. They moved slowly past the singers and the dancers, past the great fire, while everyone stood still and silent. Presently they reached what I had not noticed before in the darkness, the coffin on its high bier, built so that it faced the firelit circle. Here they stopped. The woman stepped forward alone. Then the silence about us, the silence of the night itself, was filled with her "Cry"—the sad, terrible sound of human grief, a lonely proud, noble, almost cosmic lamentation. It pierced the darkness, travelling towards the mountains, it was everywhere.

After a moment others joined in, the singers chanted softly, accompanying her lament. This was her tribute to her dead husband, this was his family's and his tribe's farewell. When it ceased there was another long silence, through which she was led gently back, between the supporting men, into the house.

This ritual moment of the Cry, with the comfort it must bring to express grief with such love, such truth, such finality, is the reason for the name of the second Dance Wovoka gave to his people, as a corollary to the Spirit Dance of the Other World, to which the departed passes, over the bridge of the Milky Way.

In that Spirit Land, Amerindians believe their dead relatives, friends, ancestors, and the Indian peoples generally, live and are in touch with the things of earth. When the still living reach the Spirit land by dancing the Ghost Dance, and passing into the trance induced by it, then messages and guidance from the ancestors and the friends and relatives can be brought back to waking consciousness.

Many believe that the two worlds are very close to one another, that they overlap and influence each other. In 1855 Chief Seathe (Seattle) expressed this belief to the white signers of the Treaty of Point Elliott:

> "Our religion is the traditions of our ancestors, the dreams of our old men, given them by the Great Spirit, and the visions of our sachems, and is written in the hearts of our people.
>
> "Every part of this country is sacred to my people. Every hillside every valley, every plain and grove has been hallowed by some fond memory or some sad experience of my tribe. . . .
>
> "The braves, fond mothers, glad-hearted maidens and even little children, who lived here. . . . still love these solitudes. Their deep fastnesses at eventide grow shadowy with the presence of dusty spirits. When the last red man shall have perished from the earth and his memory among white men shall have become a myth, these shores shall swarm with the invisible dead of my tribe . . .
>
> "At night when the streets of your cities and villages shall be silent, and you think them deserted, they will throng with the returning hosts that once filled and still love this beautiful land.
>
> "The white man will never be alone. Let him be just and deal kindly with my people, for the dead are not altogether powerless. Dead, did I say? There is no death, only a change of worlds."

In order that the newly dead may find their way quickly and surely to the Spirit land, prayers and the songs of the Cry-Dance encourage them to set out and, to help them free themselves from the ties of earth, their belongings are destroyed, so that there may be nothing tangible to hold them back.

For a time after they are buried their names are not mentioned for fear that on hearing them they might falter on their long journey, or even, bewildered, turn back to us and become earthbound.

The dancing resumed. It would continue till the dawn. When the first light began to show, the dancers turned inward toward the fire, lifted what they were holding high, higher, balanced it, and flung it on the flames. Everything came to a stop, chanting and dancing ceased. The circle broke and all went to the house. I too, went with the onlookers, for coffee and food.

The next time that I went to a Cry-Dance I was drawn into the circle to dance with the family and friends of the dead woman. I danced all night. The step easily "came back" to me. This was something I had always known. I had no separate existence. I was one with the dancers, one with the earth we trod, one with all creatures, those still here, those who had shed their human overcoats and were gone ahead.

The cloth that I held and raised and lowered with the other dancers, was part of the woman's clothing, torn into strips so that it could be distributed among many and disposed of in the fire at the end of the dance.

When I stooped to pick it up and take my place in the circle, I saw that it was part of a dress. Did she wear it on a happy or a sad occasion? Was it a familiar friendly dress worn about the house, for sweeping or for baking bread? Holding it made me feel near to her.

When at the end I turned with the others and flung it on the fire, I understood that with it would go the unhappiness, faults, failings, bad luck, bitterness, pain, not only of this woman, but of her family, her tribe, her country and the world. It is a way of cleansing the human race of some of its heavy burdens. The departing give us this last gift. As they shared what they had when they were living here, now they share the purifying fire, setting us free to continue our journey on the earth, as we help to set them free to continue on the road of the Dead to the Spirit World.

Gradually as I danced in more Cry Dances I came to feel that the ancient burial way is a good one, comforting to the bereaved and to the friends of the departed, who take actual psychic and physical part in the departure. Also it serves to draw the living together. I felt closer to my brothers and sisters after each dancing, and closer to the Grandfathers. There is a very thin line of separation between the living and the dead. Amerindians believe that direct communication with the invisible world is possible, that the living and the dead depend upon each other in ways that interact and help to maintain both worlds.

I learned, too, that though the singing and the dance steps are the same, the experience in the circle varies with the lives and characters of the people being buried. Very different from the gentle, serene vibrations I absorbed as I danced for an older woman, who had led a good life, a source of wisdom and strength to her people, were those which swept through me when I danced for a man who was an alcoholic and who died badly, and the heavy horror-filled atmosphere round the death of a woman who was found in a ditch, apparently murdered. The Cry Dance is a deep and varied experience for those who dance and those who sing.

The singers are usually older, much respected men, who remember the old ways and "have" their songs, handed down to them from earlier Singers, or received in fast, or recaptured from the Spirit World in vision trance, from those who sang them when they were still on earth.

Some of the Singers are training their grandsons and other young men, willing and able to undergo the training, to whom they will give their songs before the time comes to sing the last song. This Last Song is a personal utterance, a summary, a thanksgiving, before departing upon the Milky Way. Hartley Burr Alexander has translated a very fine one:

Let it be beautiful
When I sing the last song,
Let it be day.
I would stand upon my two feet, singing,

I would look upward with my eyes, singing,
I would have the winds to envelope my body,
I would have the sun to shine upon my body.
Let it be beautiful
When Thou wouldst slay me, O Shining One,
Let it be day when I sing the last song.

25

Tatanka-Ohitika, Sioux Medicine Man, said:

"Then I had a dream, and in my dream one of these small round stones appeared to me and told me that the maker of all was Wakan-Tanka, and that in order to honor him I must honor his works in nature. The stone said that by my search I had shown myself worthy of supernatural help. It said that if I were curing a sick person I might ask its assistance, and that all the forces of nature would help me to work a cure.

"In all my life I have been faithful to the sacred stones. I have lived according to their requirements, and they have helped me in all my troubles. I have tried to qualify myself as well as possible to handle these sacred stones, yet I know I am not worthy to speak to Wakan-Tanka. I make my request of the stones and they are my intercessors."

When I was a child I knew about stones. They were my best friends. I gathered them wherever I found them. I kept them in my pockets and slept with them under the pillow. I held them in my palms and rubbed them in my hands as I went about my day. I talked to them and was encouraged or comforted.

Later I came to know the great stone circles like Stonehenge, when it was neglected and there were no fences, and I could ride to it for the sunrise and sunset and be the only person there. I saw others, in Brittany and small ones in the Isle of Man. Lately, I have travelled widely over this continent of Turtle Island and seen many sacred stone formations.

I used to make rings of favorite stones around me and sit in the center, protected, happy. Then I discovered that others had been before me. There were circles everywhere I went, some very old, hidden beneath the underbrush, the sand, or the roots of trees, some newer, as though they had sprung up overnight. Often they only needed a little clearing work to be set free. Some had the cross of the Four Directions through the center, reminders of the Medicine Wheel, the Wheel of Creation, the Wheel of Day.

Our knowledge of the power of stones is very old. Stones appear in the Bible, and long before that, in early sacred scriptures that have come down to us precariously. Stone circles are mentioned in the Rig Veda: "I place this circle of stones for the living, it is a heap which can keep death at a distance." Stones embody the magical vibrations of the mineral world.

I received my healing stone when I was in Wyoming, after my first fast. Power Man's son, a boy of twelve or so, ran to me one day and thrust it into my hands. I thought it was a treasure that he had just found and wanted me to admire, but when I tried to hand it back to him, he signed that it was for me to keep, and went away.

It was the only time we were alone. I saw him in the distance but I never heard him speak to anyone. He was practicing for the Eagle Dance, and when I saw him later in his gorgeous authentic regalia, swooping and soaring, no boy but an eagle, I was deeply moved.

The stone he gave me was dark red, like the sacred pipestone, but a different texture, with mineral colorings through it. It was round, slightly oval on top, flattened beneath, perfectly formed for healing; an ancient stone, used by a Medicine Man, whose vibrations lingered in it. It was worn smooth by many rubbings, his, and perhaps other hands before his, until it was vibrant with power.

Now it was in my hands, but I did not realize at once that I was to *use* it. I was waiting for Power Man to bestow it on me officially. I thought that it was now a gift from a young Indian who for some reason wanted to give it to me. I took it carefully away with me and put it among my treasures. Now and then I lifted it up and held it in my hands. However cool it was to the touch my hands burned and tingled when I held it.

Presently I noticed that when I held it, or had just returned it to its place, someone would come for special help, and always at those times they felt they were helped. After awhile the point the Grandfathers were making got through to me. The stone contained the healing powers of the mineral world, the wisdom of the Medicine Men who had used it, and now I, its present custodian, opened my slowly growing channel to the healing forces flowing through it.

Gently, steadily, I was trained in the use of it, as in my other training; first, by observation—in the Sweats, the Ceremonies, the Fasts—then, by meditation on the meaning of what I observed, then by participation, then by practice, but never by communication in classes, courses, tutoring, or even the spoken word. That is not the way for some of us apparently. Now and then a hint would be dropped by Power Man, or Eagle Man, or a wise woman, but I had to be on the alert to catch it beneath quite ordinary speaking, and I was always hoping for the time to be right for me to be taught many things specifically.

I felt that I should ask for this from a Medicine Man. Tsaviaya's lodge was too far from where I lived for any regular instruction, and those who sweated in it were not too friendly to non-Indians. Power Man had stopped coming to us. We had to go to Wyoming to consult him. More and more Eagle Man had become my only Medicine Man. So I made the mistake of asking him:

"I hope you will begin to train me soon, will you, please?"

He said nothing.

I began again. "When the time is right? I know I am un-
worthy but I do desire to learn."

He looked at me quizzically.

"What do you want?"

"To learn how to be a Medicine Woman."

"I can't help you. No one can help you."

He added, as a concession to my stupidity, "You got all you
need. You got your Pipe, you been through Fast, you got your
Stone, you got your feathers."

I had never told him about the Stone, waiting for him or
someone to confer it on me, waiting for him or someone to
"train" me in the use of it. I had not told him about the feathers
that had come to me in special ways, gifts from grateful
people, or blown to my feet by the wind, after a Pipe, feathers
from the small Eagle, the Red-tailed Hawk. I had begun tentatively to use them as I did the Stone, but always in the spirit of
someone who is warming-up before the real beginning.

"The rest," he said, almost impatiently at having to use
words for things which were self-evident and better unsaid,
"is up to you."

There was a long silence. Then he smiled his rare warm
smile. He put his hand on my shoulder.

"You doing all right. Just go on. We all have to go on." He
added, "You got all you need."

I guessed at the time we spoke that others were receiving a
definite, fuller training, that there were lodges of higher degree than the ones I attended, but these were probably open
only to specially designated people, descendants of Medicine
Men or Holy Men, or those whose vision-fasts marked them out
to the Elders. I, having come late to the Indian way of life, and
being considered non-Indian, could not be of those. I also
knew that it was true, I had "got all you need," more, so much
more than I dreamed of when I took my first steps toward the
Sweat Lodge.

After this talk I understood that training on this plane while
helpful is not the most important thing. The way of develop-
ment is the way of commitment, practice and *listening*. The
real training is done by the Grandfathers teaching us within.
Slowly, surely, inner wisdom grows. It may be harder this way
but IT WORKS.

26

The day came when Eagle Man closed his Sweat Lodge to non-Indians. Because he had made his vow to run a Sweat Lodge open to all people, whatever their skins, he compromised by saying that whites might come occasionally, but only as visitors, or if they were severely ill, to be doctored.

It was like saying that people could only go to their churches occasionally or on a stretcher. The small group who had been coming to the Sweats once a week for years, and oftener when they were needed, were stunned. They had seen, without acceptance, the growing pressures on him from his Indian people to get rid of non-Indians, but those who were most vociferous seldom came to the Sweat Lodge and did not support him when he started it. From the beginning it was a small harmonious group of a few whites who joined the Indians who did "stand behind" him. The Sweat Lodge had become a part of life for them and they served it faithfully. They had done much for the community, perhaps too much. Now they were banished from their Medicine Man, their Sweat Lodge, their friends, on account of the color of their skins.

They believed they were an integral part of the Sweat Lodge. One of them was Eagle Man's adopted son, one was his Singer, others had been doorkeepers. One was his acknowledged "right hand" who travelled with him and helped him set up Sweat Lodges. Two of the men and two of the women had received their Pipes. Others were chronically ill and needed the regular and doctoring Sweats. Now they had nowhere to go.

Ironically we had prayed and sweated for more and more of Eagle Man's Indian people to swing in behind him and find in him the strong and wise leader they were looking for. We felt that we were warming the seats for those who should, and one day would, be sitting there. We did not dream that when they came it would mean the closing of the Sweat Lodge to non-Indians.

We had been surprised and hurt for some time by the growing coldness of old friends. Before the political climate changed we had shared everything together, we had gone to sunrise Sweats, Thanksgiving dinners, special gatherings. We had eaten and slept in the community house, camped, gone pi-nutting, shared our food and laughter and told each other some of our deepest experiences. Now we faced embarrassed looks, cold silences, total withdrawals. Still we believed this was a temporary political wind that would blow itself out if we were patient, and after all, the white race had this sort of treatment coming to it, "but not to *us*", we added a little smugly, for we were obviously different. Evidently it was not so obvious to the Indians. I think that hurt us most of all. But we believed in the teachings of the *Warriors of the Rainbow*.

> "Like the great Indians of old, they will teach unity, love and understanding among all people. They will listen no more to the little people who say they alone have the truth, but shall see that He Who Listens To All is too big for little things, too full of justice to accept but one self-chosen people, too free to be caged by any mind. They will listen instead ·to those who teach

harmony between all men, even as the wind blows
without favoritism into all the corners of the world."

Those were Indian words, of present day people. Surely
they would prevail, and apply to the Sweat Lodge now so
much a part of us.

I was away when Eagle Man summoned his whites to hear
their dismissal. I had gone on a mission to the East. When I
saw them again, they were gathered together to comfort each
other and to pick up the pieces "after the earthquake", one of
them said. They told me what had happened and how they
had quarreled among themselves, blaming this one and that
one for the change in Eagle Man. Bitter things were said,
people were refusing to see each other, "for awhile".

They asked me what I thought? Who was to blame? I said
that perhaps besides the obvious karmic lesson whites have
to learn of racial tolerance and brotherhood, we were also
being pulled back from complacency and taking for granted
the blessings of the Sweat Lodge. They agreed, but one of
them said to me:

"It's different for you. You can still go there. They will always accept you."

I said, "Perhaps, but I can't accept a Sweat Lodge or any
other group that is racist."

We discussed what next? I said that the Grandfathers could
be telling us not to get bogged down in any one way to the
Light. People of mixed blood, and that takes in the majority
living on this continent of Turtle Island, should go by mixed
ways to the Center, not follow one way alone. Racial and
ancestral karma allots the duty and gives the opportunity to
pass through many way-stations, faiths and disciplines, absorbing what is best in each, taking what is true in each, to
enrich our give-aways. We are meant to be bridges, inter-
preters, and yes, visitors, much as the word stings.

"I need to be part of it," the adopted son said.

"I know, but now the time seems to have come to release
Eagle Man from the burden of carrying us, being responsible
for what we do with our Pipes, having to accept our help,
alienating his Indian people because of us. Perhaps we
should give thanks for all that he has given us, all we have
learned. We must love him and let him go."

There was a heavy silence. Then the Singer said sadly:

"I thought he was my closest friend. We went to so many places and did so much together. For three years."

"I know." And I did. "He was my friend for eleven years, and my Fast Brother. He is still our brother, though we don't understand what he's going through."

"He looks terrible."

"He needs our help, but not the kind we've been giving him till now. We must try to pour out energy to him and to the others. I don't suppose we can have the least idea of what it must be like to be an Indian and come to the Sweat Lodge and find a lot of whites there! 'Here too!' Indians think, 'Can't we ever get away from *them*? And now I suppose *they'll* take over. They always do.' Even if we're not doing any of the things they dislike whites for, even if we're honestly humble and loving, we irk them. Probably our friendship irks them most of all."

They listened in silence, with here and there a comprehending nod, but they were still suffering.

"Let's think of it as a test," I said. "It must be, for all of us. No resentment, no self-pity, no hurt pride. It's a hell of a test, but it's all we can do for him and for ourselves—to pass it as well as we can."

Someone said again, "It's different for you." And another, "You didn't have to be there."

"What was the first thing you did when he told you?"

"Went out and sat beneath a tree and prayed for him. He asked us to. It was only afterwards . . ."

"I think we should do it often."

"Do what?"

"Sit under a tree and send a Voice for him, and for his people and for us."

I did not tell them that I had met my test the day before and was still reeling from the shock of it, nor that Eagle Man's last words to me were "Go and take care of the people."

27

I had come to Eagle Man that morning in some excitement, to report on the last mission, during which interesting things had happened which he would like to hear. I found him alone in the living room of his small home, not much bigger than a mining hut, but with the magic quality of expanding or shrinking its walls to contain in comfort and warm hospitality the few or the many who thronged to him, reds and whites alike, perhaps the whites more often.

His wife is wise and beautiful, mother of ten, adopted mother of more. She radiated love. This was the place we all came to, to share the high and low points of our lives, and I must have bounced in merrily, hands outstretched.

He did not take them. He did not smile. He did not look at me. His face was drawn and grim, the face of a hostile stranger. His voice when he spoke was harsh and loud.

"You won't like what I say. I'm going to stamp on your toes. Give me your Pipe. You been misusing it."

If he had run me through with a spear I couldn't have been more shocked. A sharp pain went through my solar plexus. I wasn't armored against a psychic wound, in this place, from this man. I had never imagined needing protection from Eagle Man. I stared at him dazed.

He shouted, "Give me your Pipe."

I said, "Why?"

He said, "never mind why! You been using it wrong. You been showing off."

Then anger came and outrage. I forgot that one must not interrupt nor contradict a Medicine Man. I found some sort of voice to protest, "That isn't true!"

"Don't argue," he said, "just give me your Pipe."

With hatred, with scorn! My friend, my Fast-Brother, my Medicine Man! The one who, of all others, knew what the Pipe was to me.

He stepped toward me, strong and menacing. All certainties, all comforts were gone from this familiar place. It was a chasm of violence and terror, into which I would fall, when I had finished bleeding. . . . I didn't remember to call to the Grandfathers for help. I couldn't think of anything, but from somewhere far away, a spark of strength stood up in me to say:

"No. I won't give you my Pipe."

Not like this. Not in hatred and contempt.

I thought he was going to strike me, and tardily I brought up my frail shield. But it was too late to ward off the grim doubts rushing in. Had I misused the Pipe? Had I tried to get something for myself I shouldn't ask for? Had I shown off to people? I didn't think so. I found more strength to say:

"I can't give you my Pipe. It isn't mine to give. It belongs to the Great Spirit."

His face changed. Something came back from wherever it had gone. His eyes were almost the eyes I knew. I spoke to them, with tremulous breath, all the while bleeding, bleeding . . .

"You made my Pipe and I shall always be thankful, but you didn't give it to me. Power Man gave it to me. He blessed it in his Sweat."

This seemed to enrage him again.

"I don't care what Power Man did! Give me your Pipe!"

"I can't." I pleaded, as if he *must* understand, "it isn't mine to give."

I closed my eyes. I was feeling dizzy. I thought I might faint, but I forced my human envelope to hold me up, straight and facing him. There was a long silence. A series of pictures were crossing my closed eyelids: Eagle Man wrapped in his blue towel, bringing two pails of water to the Sweat Lodge, nodding, smiling, loving all the world; Eagle Man, kneeling before the altar, filling his Pipe, a silhouette of dignified humility; Eagle Man fastening me in for the Fast; Eagle Man pointing to the Red-tailed Hawk circling above us, and telling me that it was mine—that time I had heard the silent communication, but there were many times I must have missed. Was this horror that was happening to us coming from a long lack of communication? Eagle Man whom I doctored, whom I assisted, whom I travelled with; Eagle Man whom I loved and trusted, as I thought he loved and trusted me.

I heard my voice protesting again, unsteadily, "I have not misused my Pipe. I have not used it for show-off or myself. It is sacred. I say this to you and to the Grandfathers."

I willed myself to look at him, and so we stood, facing each other, questioningly. There was a change in the room now. I saw that he believed me. He said, more gently,

"Go and get the Pipe."

I waited for a moment, until my knees would move, then I wobbled to the door and started toward the car. Everything was still out of focus. The distance seemed immense, the ground strange, I walked through a muddy, resistant sea. As I went I remembered a day long ago, on the mountain, when he talked about himself, telling many things—one I had forgotten till this moment—that Power Man once "got mad" and demanded his Pipe, and he had resisted and refused, saying Power Man did not give it to him. It came from another, older Medicine Man. "And if that man had asked for it?" "Then I'd have had to give it. Then it would have been for real." He described his suffering, his doubts, the despair, the rejection, the opening beneath him which he called "a cleft."

Now he had done to me what Power Man did to him. If Power
Man had asked me for my Pipe, it would have been "for real"
and for good reason. This, then, was not. This, then, was a
test. I began to understand.

I climbed into the car, brought out the bowl of sage and
smudged myself. Then I sent a Voice, for help, for guidance.

There was one Indian prayer I loved. I said it now:

"Father, a needy one stands before Thee. I that sing am he."

After awhile of centering, and donning belatedly my armor,
I walked slowly back. I found him standing where I left him, in
the middle of the room. We looked at each other. I saw that he
knew what I had been doing in the car. I saw that he believed
me, and perhaps he always had. I took the Pipe out of its Bag
and presented it to him 'in a sacred manner'.

He took it from me, ritually. He wiped it over with a long
piece of sage that he had ready on a table beside him. Then he
smudged it with burning sweet grass. He handed it back to
me, and motioned toward the Bag. He smudged that too, took
the Pipe and put it in, tying up the ends in the special, sym-
metrical way I could never master.

Then he straightened himself and smiled.

"Well," he said, "you done your part."

But sadness came with understanding. When he smudged
the Pipe, he had cut the ties between us. Something was gone
that could not be restored. My Pipe was no longer "under
Eagle Man's Pipe." This was Graduation, a long-worked-for
achievement, but a rough and lonely one.

I said what was left to be said:

"Thank you for all that you have done and all that I have
learned, and for blessing this Pipe and cleansing it from my
mistakes."

His wife came from the kitchen, where she must have heard
everything, and perhaps had prayed for us. She greeted me
warmly and looked at me, concerned.

"Sit down now and have coffee."

I said that I must go. I said "another time," for I wanted them
to know that I would be back.

"That's right," Eagle Man said, "go and take care of the
people."

We embraced, and I went out, weeping.

That night I took my Pipe up on the mountain, to smoke beside the stream. There I wept again. But after awhile I filled it with the tobacco Eagle Man had given me, and held it stem first to the stars.

"Great One, I send a Voice . . ."

Then I began to smoke, and everything smoked with me.

Epilogue

Many seasons later I came back to Eagle Man's Sweat Lodge, and now and then I go there when the time is right. Some of the white group also returned. Eagle Man said it was "like old times", but even as he said it, we knew that could not be. Doors had closed between us, new doors opened. Still, we were there again, sitting in the circle, and we would come again sometimes as visitors.

The Grandfathers understand *intent*. If They are sometimes dismayed or perhaps amused, at the strange channels offered to Their use, They never fail in courtesy, reassuring us with signs and sounds that we are not alone; unique, but not alone.

The more we practice what we have come to know, the more we use all that the Great Spirit has given to us to be used in the service and for the healing of others, the more we *live* what we know, the more we realize that Wakan-Tanka, Great Mystery , has given latent powers to his children. If we *willed* harmlessness and joy, we might all be Medicine Men,

Medicine Women, Medicine children, called to take care of each other, called to little and great miseries, called, especially, to cleanse the pollution and staunch the wounds of our Mother Earth.

Great Spirit,
Whose voice we hear in the winds,
Whose breath gives life to the world,
we would restore what greed
has taken from the Earth.

Great Spirit,
we are blind and deaf.
Open your eyes to us
that we may see.
open your ears in us
that we may hear compassion
open your compassion in us
that we may have compassion
upon the Earth,
upon our Mother Earth.

Great Spirit,
may our feet walk gently,
may our hands respect her,
may we learn the lessons
in every leaf and rock,
may our strength restore her.

Great Spirit,
When we face the sunset
when we come singing
the last song, may it be
without shame, singing
'it is finished in beauty,
it is finished in beauty!'

The means of contacting the spiritual element in your nature are varied. It may be accomplished through a group encounter as was done by Evelyn Eaton. Or, it may be accomplished directly through a mystical experience as related by AE (George William Russell) in his Quest book autobiography

THE CANDLE OF VISION

Or through dreams and fantasy as "diaried" in

AND A TIME TO DIE
by Marc Pelgrin

Through meditation as taught in the Quest book

MEDITATION
by Adelaide Gardner

Through devotion as in the Quest book

TRUST YOURSELF TO LIFE
by Clara Codd

Or, through the pure love of life as pictured in the Quest book

DO YOU SEE WHAT I SEE?
by Jae Jah Noh

Available from
QUEST BOOKS
306 W. Geneva Road
Wheaton, Illinois 60187